The Millennial's Guide to

Making Happiness

Coming Soon by Chris Butsch:

ASAP Happiness: 25 Ways to Build Happiness in 5 Minutes

The Millennial's Guide to Making Happiness, Volume II

The Millennial's Guide to

Making Happiness

VOLUME I

CHRIS BUTSCH

**BOOK**LOGIX®
Alpharetta, GA

Copyright © 2016 by Chris Butsch

ISBN: 978-1-61005-842-1

Library of Congress Control Number: 2016918783

10 9 8 7 6 5 4 3 2   1 2 0 2 1 6

Printed in the United States of America

∞This paper meets the requirements of ANSI/NISO Z39.48-1992 (Permanence of Paper)

Cover art by Erin Tyler
Illustrations by Joshua McGill

*To everyone who's had a conversation with me about happiness,
and Mom and Dad, for bringing me the most.*

Happiness is not something ready-made. It comes from your own actions.

—His Holiness the 14th Dalai Lama

Contents

Chapter 6—Mindfulness: Moment-to-Moment Happiness

Introduction

We're in This Together

Life is a storm, my young friend. You will bask in the sunlight one moment, be shattered on the rocks the next. What makes you a man is what you do when that storm comes.
—Edmond Dantes, from Alexandre Dumas's
The Count of Monte Cristo

As we grew up, we were taught how to tie our shoes, perform basic arithmetic, and how to pronounce "colonel." Later, we learned about hippos, Hitler, and hydrogen; herpes, humanities, and H. G. Wells.

Yet there's another topic of significantly greater importance we gloss over, so important our Founding Fathers listed its pursuit as our third inalienable right. We learn plenty about life and liberty, so why do we enter the adult world knowing so little about happiness?

As we're eventually cast into the sea of real life to battle the heaving waves of circumstance, luck, and providence, we often find ourselves tossed around with little control. Some days we question what we're sailing toward. Other days we just try to stay afloat.

We Millennials are the most educated, diverse, and progressive generation in our nation's history. As such, we're the most capable generation ever to reverse the trends of depression, greed, and addiction plaguing our society, and ignite a happiness revolution that our Founding Fathers would be proud of. All we need is a guide to build our own happy lives and spread that happiness to others like wildfire.

I've done my best to write precisely that guide. The science and stories you're about to read are the culmination of one Millennial's quest to understand happiness better than most people triple my age (or so they tell me!). I've read more science than Bill Nye on Adderall, traveled to more exotic locales than a *Fast and Furious* scouting agent, and disappointed Buddhist monks with my lame basketball skills, all on a worldwide hunt for happiness. And where my own knowledge or expertise fell short, I talked to people smarter than me: psychologists, researchers, gurus, swamis, millionaires, monks, and Millennials—thousands of us.

The most poignant moment of my happiness quest came on a frosty morning at Magnolia Grove Monastery in Mississippi, where I'd ventured on my journey to study mindfulness and meditation. Among the nonmonastic long-term residents was a boy named Kian, who, after years of bullying by his classmates and abuse by his father, had been diagnosed with PTSD at age fifteen. Since his mother lacked the resources for traditional psychological counseling, the monks offered to let Kian live with them in peace.

Though I'd done my best to conceal my status as a researching author, I blew my cover one morning when Kian spied the title of my book over my shoulder as I typed. "Can I read some of it?" he asked.

"Sure, man. Want to read what I've just finished?" I said, scrolling to the top of the section on caffeine in the pleasure chapter.

At that moment, Brother Harmony (who you'll meet later) came in to ask if we'd care to join him on a mindful walk. As I scanned the ground for my missing left glove, Kian repositioned my laptop in front of himself and began intently scanning the text. "You all go ahead. I'm going to stay here and read this."

When Brother Harmony and I returned from our stroll, Kian—and my laptop—were gone. I fully trusted him and there was no Wi-Fi for shenanigans, so I thought nothing of it.

Lunch passed, then afternoon meditation, then English class, and nobody had seen Kian all day. As the brothers and sisters prepared for dinner, Brother Harmony and I decided to visit the men's dorm and check on him. But before I could lace up my left boot, Kian appeared in the doorway to the kitchen, laptop under his arm and face rouged with emotion.

"Sorry . . . I, uh, read the whole thing," he said. He then placed my laptop on the table, walked toward me, and gripped me in the tightest hug I've ever felt. "Reading your book was the first time I've laughed and felt hope in months."

The moment Kian embraced me instilled in me the gravity of my undertaking. Using my penchant for research and semi-decent writing skills, I had to publish a positive psychology book for young people not only good enough to reach you and your friends, but the other Kians of the world whom I may never meet.

My promise to them, and to you, is that I've done my absolute best to write that book. So, please enjoy *The Millennial's Guide to Making Happiness*, Volume I.

Meet Your Author!

Life is full of suffering. If we don't have enough happiness on reserve, we have no way to take care of our despair.
—Thich Nhat Hanh

This isn't a section about how "I'm the typical Millennial and that's why you should listen to me." By definition, we're an atypical generation. Unburdened by war or segregation, we've brought a whirlwind of progressive thought and technological advances to this country together. We've connected the world through social media and an unprecedented fascination with international travel. Despite our diversity, we've bonded through the fallout of the financial crisis, and we embrace and even revel in our status as a misunderstood generation.

Instead, this book begins with the story of one Millennial's struggle for happiness; how I spent my teens and twenties earning a ticket to the American Dream, only to freefall into the throes of depression seemingly overnight.

From the beginning, I was on track for a happy life. I was born and raised in Atlanta, Georgia, by my loving father, a banker, and mother, a writer. I have one sister, Catherine, who's three years older. I call her Sistopher.

Blessed with decent gray matter, I maintained pretty strong grades throughout school, earning a place in one of Georgia's best high schools. Perhaps to balance out the above-average brainpower, God decided to make me look like an Aryan Napoleon Dynamite in high school, so I excelled academically, totally undistracted by female attention.

I felt briefly depressed in tenth grade simply because I felt academics were my only contribution to society. Joining the Community Service Club, and later serving as captain, put a swift end to my despondence. Who could feel depressed while building a Habitat for Humanity home with your friends?

By the time senior year rolled around I had amassed a small fortune in AP credits and community service hours, ready to supplicate college recruiters. In December, the night before my AP French Bible semester exam, I ran through my neighborhood like a horseless Paul Revere, waving in my hand an acceptance letter from Vanderbilt University.

In 2009 I began freshman year at Vandy, where right away I felt empowered by my big-brained colleagues. In the spring, I read a *Forbes* article on how the business world desperately needed more young-blood bilinguals fluent in both technology and business, so I designed a custom major in engineering management. It wasn't much fun, but I felt I should invest my exorbitant tuition in something potentially lucrative.

Free from the oppression of back-to-back AP classes, in college I hosted a radio show, found a fashion sense, and gained thirty pounds of muscle. My substantial visual upgrade and practiced radio voice garnered me some fresh attention from the fairer sex, though joining a fraternity turned many of them away again.

Overall, though, life in college was pretty sweet. I maintained good grades and spent my weekends surrounded by debauchery, checking all the boxes of a modern-day Dionysus. Convert a pickup truck into a hot tub? Check. Throw a couch out of a window? Check. Streak with the hipsters? Check, check, check.

But despite the overwhelming fun, I could sense depression nibbling at the edges of my psyche again. *Why?* I decided to fall back on a proven cure and became my fraternity's community service chair, cooking for halfway houses and hazing pledges by dragging them to 7:00 a.m. Habitat for Humanity outings on Saturdays.

The balance of partying, studying, and volunteering created a fragile happiness equilibrium that carried me through college. But I couldn't shake the feeling of temporariness, like I'd found happiness partying on the beach while the sea of real life beckoned. So by the middle of my junior year, I felt eager to try building a happy life in the crucible of the adult world.

During the summer of 2012 I interned at the Nashville Entrepreneur Center, where I bolstered my networking skills tenfold and met many of the sages you'll hear from in this book. After a grueling, nail-biting interview process in the fall, I landed a job with healthcare IT giant Epic based in Madison, Wisconsin. To loosen the financial noose on my family, I squeezed my last few credits into my fall term and graduated a semester early.

Then, in the spring of 2013, I crammed my life into my compact sedan and journeyed north, bracing for my initiation into the adult world.

Far from a D-Day landing, my first days as a real adult were even better than college. Soon I was surrounded by hundreds of other gifted new-hire Millennials at the equivalent of Healthcare Hogwarts, gleefully learning our trade from quirky teachers who excused us well before five o'clock. Each day after "work," we'd bask lakeside under the Midwestern summer sun, cracking open Wisconsin craft beers to chat minutia like the day's lunch menu and the best bars in town.

Though my tanning efforts continued to yield little fruit, I felt tremendously accomplished. After seventeen years of busting my butt in classrooms, standardized tests, and interviews, I had made it. I'd crossed a finish line.

As training wrapped up and the real work began, life only got better. Though a brutal Wisconsin winter caused me to shiver vigorously enough to qualify as dancing, I stayed warm beside new friends, cheese curds, and my first bonus. My project was going well, and my clients generously shared positive feedback to my superiors, who rewarded my dedication with checks, steaks, and flight upgrades. My manager had her own special way of sharing her approval; each time I kicked ass, she'd send a pic of The Fonz flashing a thumbs-up. So at the end of a hard day's work, I counted my Fonzes like war medals, feeling a surge of motivation to get up and do it all again tomorrow.

The positive feedback didn't come cheap, though. I later calculated that during my first year at Epic, I worked an average of sixty-nine hours a week, not including time I spent in the air flying my way to Gold status in two airlines. I passed out from exhaustion so often without brushing my teeth that I even got a few cavities. My dentist told me, "I bet I know where *you* work. Couldn't resist those subsidized energy drinks?" I denied her the satisfaction, but between us, Cherry AMP was my favorite, followed by Monster Assault. Red Bull wasn't cost effective.

But all the time and tooth decay were worth it. Prior to work, life had been a whirlwind of uncertainty—apply to the right schools, take the right classes, network here and there . . . all leading up to this: my first job. I could finally focus all of my time and energy on *one* thing, and kick ass and make bank doing it.

As the snow melted, my ego and bank account inflated. I could afford nicer things, so I recklessly indulged in a bigger TV, an Xbox One, *and* a PlayStation 4. I ate and drank whatever I wanted, drove a fast car, and rented an impressive apartment that I made a habit of filling with friends and cute girls—the kind who wouldn't have even lent a pencil to me in high school.

And this was just the beginning. Soon, my boss offered me a promotion and handed me a hefty check. She might as well have handed me a first-class ticket to the American Dream. *This is it*, I remember thinking one night, as I powered through my last unread emails from the day. *I'm going to be one of society's winners.*

As I relished in the thought, I opened my last unread email to see The Fonz flashing me a thumbs-up.

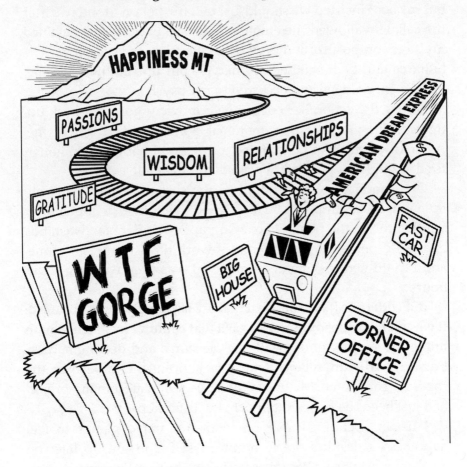

Three weeks later I was diagnosed with clinical depression. What had happened in three weeks? Had I lost my job? A loved one? Nope. That's the scary part: *nothing* had happened.

Well, almost nothing.

Due to a miscommunication with my client, I had received scathing feedback from one of the hospital's managers. For damage control and to sate the client's bloodlust, I was immediately removed from the project, my reputation shattered.

I was getting ready for a night out with friends on Friday evening when I received the news from my boss. Naturally, I was dumbfounded and crushed. It felt like a sudden breakup in a healthy relationship. I squeaked out a few "whys" and "hows," but my boss insisted we should just talk further on Monday. After the call, I swallowed the emotional nausea back down, regained my stoic composure, and even made it out to see my friends. The billiards and beer soothed my nerves, but unbeknownst to me, permanent damage had occurred to my psyche.

So like the action hero of my own movie, I got right back up, figuring I'd just had the emotional wind knocked out of me. Again, it wasn't like I'd suffered a tragedy. I hadn't even gotten fired, though the possibility was still on the table.

On Monday, my boss admitted the situation wasn't entirely my fault. I was simply to be reassigned to another customer after a little time in the penalty box. On paper, the damage wasn't as bad as I'd perceived. My friends at work thought no less of me, and I continued making good money. I was even working fewer hours.

But with time it became clear that my happiness wasn't bruised; it was pierced, bleeding from a gash that couldn't be patched with money. It seemed underneath the pleasures and fleeting success I'd surrounded myself with, my *true* happiness had been on the ropes for some time. My unceremonious removal from my project had just been the knockout punch. I was broken.

I began spending more on food and video games to feel happiness. I drank more to numb myself, and got up later on weekends. At work I became an effective but soulless automaton, heavily reliant on a daily dose of energy shots washed down with energy drinks. When I went out with friends, I had to make a forced effort to act like my old, jovial self, like an actor playing Chris in a made-for-TV movie. I wasn't happy or sad, just numb.

Since mental-health sessions were covered under my health plan, I figured I better investigate what was going on. The psych clinic first had me take an SAT-length self-evaluation with questions like, *On a scale of 1–5, how happy are you right now, 5 being the happiest?* I bubbled in plenty of 1s and 2s, but a handful of 4s and 5s as well, so I figured I wasn't suffering from Kurt Cobain levels of depression.

The first shrink I saw, a soft-spoken Midwestern woman in a handmade beige vest, broke the news to me. The test was baited to catch people trying to fake their way to a Prozac prescription by marking all 1s and 2s, and I had answered *just* realistically enough to be believable, yet highly concerning. A psychiatrist, psychologist, and therapist all made room to see me that week. Clearly, something bad was going on.

In July of 2014, the head of the department, a thin-haired Minnesotan with a clip-on bow tie, issued my final diagnosis: clinical depression. Given I was still a functioning member of society, my therapy squad decided we'd just let time and drugs heal me.

So that evening, at age twenty-three, I joined 10 percent of America and began taking an antidepressant.

With time, things only got worse. By September it became clear that my depression wasn't going to expire on its own. On my birthday, surrounded by close friends and family, I opened presents with the ecstasy one feels when doing their taxes. In October I began suffering from a lesser-known side effect of depression: I lost my sense of taste.

But the worst news came in November, when I learned that my grandfather, my lifetime hero, had been diagnosed with terminal cancer. In response to this news, I felt absolutely nothing. I was back to work in seconds.

The only time I felt emotion was while listening to music. Certain songs or even notes would trigger me to burst into tears. Sometimes while driving on the highway I'd daydream about driving into the oncoming lane. For work, I often flew through freak blizzards causing violent turbulence, and even as the flight attendants clutched their seats in fear, I'd sit calmly and dispassionately, contemplating how little I'd care if the wings broke off.

Again, I wasn't sad, just numb. I didn't care about anything; looking back, I'm not even sure how I got work done. **To best describe how I felt, my emotions had previously been like a** symphony orchestra playing a mix of highs and lows throughout my life. Becoming depressed was like having the conductor walk offstage. Certain emotions would come in at weird times, while others wouldn't play their sweet music at all.

My only form of respite came in a transparent amber tube that I kept in my backpack at all times. But the Wellbutrin pills provided only a brief happiness high in the way coffee provides wakefulness. Sensing my growing dependence on the little blue bastards, I began doing some research to make sure they wouldn't cause me to grow extra nose hair or kill my mojo. Eyes half-open on a Sunday night, I dispassionately browsed WebMD and Wikipedia with waning interest, ready to unpause Netflix and resume my living coma.

Then, I stumbled upon a fact that caused me to cancel my prescription. And no, it wasn't that Wellbutrin users grow a third nipple.

This is what I read: The CDC estimates that from 1988 to 2011, antidepressant use in America increased by 400 percent. Like a bloodhound on a new trail, I soon sniffed out that by the Earth Institute at Columbia University's measure, America's happiness has been dropping since 2005.[1], [2] Clearly our penchant for pharmaceuticals isn't working. *What happened to our happiness?*

I was certain there must be better ways to build happiness. So that night, I quit Wellbutrin cold turkey, challenging myself to find them.

In the following weeks, I became my own first guinea pig, researching and practicing ways to mend my psyche with supposed "true" sources of happiness. During precious windows of free time in the air and on weekends, I read books, articles, scientific papers, religious texts, and even watched "feel good" movies to extrapolate the meaning of happiness.

A newfound sense of purpose alone was enough to stop the emotional bleeding. To accelerate my healing, I unplugged my anesthetics; no more Xbox, no more junk food, and I cut my drinking down to a few social beers per week. To further shift gears, I reignited my exercise regimen, began eating healthier, and continued reading and training my mind. I'd always wanted to learn how to cook but had made excuses for years, so one Saturday morning I invited eight of my friends to a dinner party for *that night*. Once they RSVPed, I had two choices: learn to make a delicious dish, or face the wrath of eight hungry Wisconsinites as I called Dominos in shame.

Thankfully, my chicken risotto was a hit, so I continued hosting brunch and dinner parties to reconnect with friends I'd estranged on my work warpath.

Within months I felt happier than I'd ever felt on Wellbutrin. And despite the ups and downs of everyday life, I woke up noticeably happier each day.

However, like a jealous lover, my job began pulling me away from my happiness self-training. My newfound happiness boosted my efficiency and my team's morale, but it was a one-way relationship. Work seemed to slowly syphon my happiness, not augment it. So when rumors of my impending promotion turned to fact, I faced a challenging crossroad.

During my tenure there, Epic was infamous for having the acceptance rate of the Navy SEALs and the retention rate of Stalin's Red Army. It hired and fired in droves, and for those who graduated from the chopping block, staying for the long haul was often a no-brainer. My promotion would come with a hike in status and an extra digit on my paycheck, but in return, I risked being horsewhipped into a high-performing psychosis . . . again. The hours seemed to *increase* with each rung of the corporate ladder at Epic, as evidenced by the gray-streaked hair, red eyes, and choked calendars of the upper ranks I'd soon join.

As I dithered about the decision, I began revealing details about my homegrown happiness to my friends, and how money and pleasure had blinded my pursuit of this "true" happiness. I felt embarrassed to admit that I had been "happiness challenged" for so long, as if I was confessing to a glaring lack of elementary knowledge like how to pay rent or change a tire.

In reality, the friends I spoke with, from starving musicians to hedge-fund managers, grad students to hip-hop artists, shared a disturbingly common reaction to my happiness revelations. They all wanted to know how I did it, how I'd found such happiness in modern society before my twenty-fifth birthday. As the emotional defenses came down, I worryingly recognized in many lifelong friends the familiar symptoms of depression.

When all along I thought I'd been behind the happiness curve, my friends insisted I was ahead. Once I realized that, all I wanted to do was catch them up. So for the first time, I felt comfortable *sharing* what I'd learned: my practices, my positive psychology research, *everything* that worked. Most importantly, I began encouraging friends new and old to join me on true happiness-building activities like volunteering, exercise, and travel. Bringing fifteen friends to a Habitat for Humanity build and seeing their looks of satisfaction and joy at our progress still serves as one of my happiest memories.

Back at work, the promotion offer sizzled on my desk. Before me stood the gateway to the American Dream, behind it every traditional metric of happiness and success I'd pursued since middle school. Should I accept the promotion, within two years I could afford my dream car, a BMW M3. Five years and I could put a down payment on a house on the shores of Lake Monona. The gateway to my old version of bliss glowed before me, and on my desk sat the key.

But a different path also lay before me. I felt there really was something to this happiness training I'd been doing. With pretty minor lifestyle variations, I'd cured my own depression, built a healthier mind and body, and helped my friends do the same. Could this sapling of happiness I'd planted provide the oxygen I'd need to climb the corporate ladder? Or had I uncovered a more meaningful purpose helping others plant their own?

So in August of 2015, just shy of my quarter-life crisis, I entered my boss's office to politely turn down my promotion. I was upfront about my plans to study happiness full time and share what I found with absolutely everyone I could reach.

His response rang with familiarity: "Come back and tell me what you find."

The first step in my quest to master happiness was admitting to myself that *I know nothing, Jon Snow*. I'd gained a foothold in happiness and found a few things that worked, but to become the Neil deGrasse Tyson of happiness for our generation, I'd need to explore other cultures, continue ravenous research, and talk to people way smarter and more important than me.

One thing was for damn sure: I'd need to leave Madison, Wisconsin.

After cramming my things into a friend's basement, I departed on an odyssey through China and Vietnam, two countries with notably slipping happiness levels, to understand the root causes of nationwide unhappiness. Then, I bounced to Mexico to investigate how our neighbor, a country racked by drug violence and corruption, still ranks higher than America in the UN's World Happiness Report.

From rice paddies to tequila farms, penthouses to shantytowns, I spoke to everyone I could about the meaning of true happiness. A Vietnamese pig farmer showed me scars from American bullets with the pride of a tattoo collector. A cabbie in Cozumel extended me an offer to marry the prettiest of his three daughters (*"Then take the uglier two to America for your friends!"*).

As my own happiness swelled, I continued my blissful quest in America, where I zigzagged the country interviewing everyone from wealth-management CEOs to dreadlocked sweat-lodge gurus, Buddhist monks to Hindu spirit guides, diehard bodybuilders to devout vegans, millionaire startup moguls to children's book authors, and soft-spoken nuns to fully nude festival-goers. I connected with hundreds of authors, psychologists, social scientists, mindfulness experts, and of course, thousands of Millennials like you and me to both collect and share wisdom, doing my best to spread the seeds of happiness in my wake.

Now I've become more fluent in happiness, able to read, write, and speak this formerly foreign language. Having rebuilt my life around what I've learned, I've reached levels of joy I'd never thought possible. Just a year ago, I'd spontaneously cry with alarming frequency. Now, I laugh and smile for no reason with the same regularity.

My pragmatic life skills have risen in tandem with my jovial demeanor. In my journeys, I've learned firsthand that a mind at peace is a powerful one. My happiness has augmented my focus, attention, energy, memory, critical thinking, listening skills, and even physical abilities. **Happiness isn't just a luxury or a one-dimensional mood upswing. It fundamentally remixes your neural chemistry into a sparkling success cocktail; it's the high-octane fuel speeding you toward a *much* better life.**

Now, I want you to get ahead of the happiness curve with me. Since we may never meet, I've done my best to pack everything into Volumes I and II of *The Millennial's Guide to Making Happiness* and the short eBook *ASAP Happiness: 25 Ways to Build Happiness in 5 Minutes.*

I'm so tremendously excited to share this knowledge with you.

The State of the Union's Happiness

So while my studies of happiness have redefined my life's course, they've also revealed a darker truth about finding happiness in Western society. That truth is this: the seeds for a truly happy life aren't sewn into our culture like they are in others. The traditional definition of happiness we grow up with is a fallacy skewed by capitalism and propagated by an agenda-driven media. As a result, many of us build our lives into houses of cards chasing this synthetic happiness, only to curl in malnourishment later in life.

Thanks to our skeptical view of the status quo, our generation is beginning to ask questions about the true sources of happiness. Problem is, we aren't really sure where to look. And while we may stumble upon *some* ways to build happiness, the broad strokes of life satisfaction continue to elude us, even into our fifties and sixties. Our siloed approaches to discovering happiness in Western society lead to too many of us living well below our potentials. Throughout our lives, most of our decisions aren't based upon building happiness, but avoiding misery. **We spend most of our life discovering things that *don't* make us happy, so why not learn about and frontload the things that *do*?**

A positive-psychology movement has always existed in our culture to some degree, but until recently the teachings have been largely retroactive and taught a generation too late. Most of the material out there centers around Baby Boomers, postulating why the divorce rate is sky-high and why job satisfaction is so low, and their conclusions often boil down to "Oh well, too late now, so pop a Viagra and buy a sailboat. *Bon(er) voyage!*"

In the movie *It's a Wonderful Life*, George Bailey's guardian angel teaches him about the value of gratefulness and self-reflection, but only once the father of four is about to jump off a bridge. In Dante's *Divine Comedy*, our protagonist is stalked by ambition, lust, and greed during a midlife crisis. His only escape is through Hell, where he witnesses "sinners" who never chose a valuable goal in life.

Why didn't anyone teach George and Dante how to be happy *earlier* in life?

As we gradually enter real life through college and our first jobs, a period scientists are calling "emerging adulthood," our happiness is like a bird leaving the nest for the first time, desperately trying to take flight before hitting the cold, hard ground (like mine did). But life doesn't have to be that way. We can train to fly now, so that as we continue facing the challenges of the adult world, we can stay aloft and soar into the blue sky.

That's why I've paused during my own emerging adulthood to write our flight manual. The concepts in this book kick-start a productive, fulfilling, and happy life. And while many of the stories are for and by Millennials, the underlying concepts are universal. Whether you're fifteen or eighty-five, I want to help you reach your blue sky.

So I've strived to make this book fun to read, full of goofy anecdotes, tearjerkers, intriguing science, and clear follow-ups. My goal was to do right by the amazing pioneers in modern positive psychology and the wonderful, wise people who opened up to me during my own journey to happiness. I sincerely hope you enjoy the book, and if you have any comments or feedback, please contact me on my website, www.chrisbutsch.com, or find me on social media. I'd genuinely love to hear from you.

How to Read This Book

The brain, the organ of experience, through which our entire lives can be led, can be trained. Happiness is a skill.
—Dan Harris, author of *10% Happier*

While I've done my best to make this book fun to read, when all's said and done it's a self-help book. To become happier, you'll take steps in your own life to implement the concepts in each chapter. **To simply read this book and put it down would be like buying a bagel, staring at it for five hours, and wondering why you're still hungry.**

To help you, I've added bullet points summarizing the takeaways from each chapter. These are not substitutes for reading the whole chapter, otherwise I would've just printed them on a T-shirt to sell in Urban Outfitters and wouldn't have bothered with the whole "book" part in the middle. Rather, the bullet points are just quick reference material to circle back to so you can stay sharp on your own happiness journey.

References:

1) Szalavitz, Maia. "What Does a 400% Increase in Antidepressant Use Really Mean?" *TIME*, October 20, 2011. Accessed October 16, 2016.
http://healthland.time.com/2011/10/20/what-does-a-400-increase-in-antidepressant-prescribing-really-mean/.

2) Schulte, Brigid. "Why the U.S. Rating on the World Happiness Report Is Lower Than It Should Be–and How to Change It." *Washington Post*, May 11, 2015.
https://www.washingtonpost.com/news/inspired-life/wp/2015/05/11/why-many-americans-are-unhappy-even-when-incomes-are-rising-and-how-we-can-change-that/.

Coming Up in Chapter 1:

- How the American Dream stunted our happiness
- What the American Dream means to migrant Millennials
- Scandinavia's secret weapon of happiness
- The 2008 financial crisis's world-changing silver lining

Chapter 1
Why We're So Unhappy

If you're reading this book, it's probably because you realize you could, and *should*, be happier. But before we dive into the solution, it's worth understanding where much of our unhappiness stems from. If you're eager to jump into the practical advice laid out in this book, by all means, hop over to Chapter 2. But if you're like me and like to understand the root of a problem first and learn a little history, this chapter is for you.

In America, we live in one of the richest, safest, and freest countries on Earth. We have a military protecting us that could yell "PULL!", launch a pigeon to the moon, and shoot it. We have the freedom to join the Church of the Flying Spaghetti Monster, vote for Kanye on a presidential ballot, and drive from Maine to SoCal without being stopped by men in fezzes demanding our papers and a bribe. We live on the world's freest playground: arable soil for planting the seeds of a happy life.

Yet, in the 2015 United Nation's World Happiness Report, which ranks the happiest countries in the world, we didn't even break into the top ten. We ranked fifteenth, below Israel, Costa Rica, and, as mentioned, *Mexico*. Yup, a country with regions racked by drug violence and decapitations still *averaged* happier than us. By 2016 we'd crept up in the rankings a little bit to thirteenth, but still can't touch the Northern Europeans or Canadians. To my British friends reading this, you all trail behind us at twenty-third, below our Irish friends at nineteenth.[1]

So if America is fertile ground for happiness, why is so little growing? Well, according to researchers, psychologists, and my Uncle David after a holiday cocktail, American culture uniquely

1

aligns us toward goals that provide little true happiness. Bourbon eggnog aside, he's exactly right.

Where did these dead-end happiness ideals come from? What can we learn from the ethos of a *much* happier country?

Abandon the American Dream

It's called the American Dream because you have to be asleep to believe it.

—Comedian George Carlin

One pervasive ideal that has defined success and happiness for generations of Americans has been the American Dream. What is it, where did it come from, and what does it mean to our generation? Is it really guiding anyone in our generation toward success and happiness, or is it time for us to define a *new* American Dream?

The American Dream is our nation's ethos that we're free to work hard toward prosperity. Unlike other doctrines that planted the seeds of our culture like the Declaration of Independence and the Constitution, the American Dream was never explicitly written down. Rather, it exists as a translucent ideal that evolves with each generation. After twenty rounds, the game of Transgenerational Telephone has resulted about as expected; immigrants first coined the term in the mid-1800s to describe the freedoms we enjoy in this country. Now, 41 percent of Americans say the American Dream is "impossible for most to achieve."[2]

So, what happened? **Clearly today's definition of the American Dream has changed since our great-great-great-grandparents eagerly awaited to have their foreign names butchered on Ellis Island (*Butsch? Butts . . . ch . . . Yeah, you're "Bush" forever now. NEXT IN LINE!*).**

To better understand how our nation's ethos has changed over time, let's jump back to its inception. And before I lose my international audience, I'd implore everyone overseas to keep reading. You'll get a sound bite of our wild history and learn a few of our dirty little secrets. I'll wager you'll see some similarities between our countries' tales of dwindling happiness.

The Birth of an Ethos

In a world gripped by old-school political thought and oppressive caste systems, outsiders longed for the unprecedented liberties we enjoyed in this country. In the March Revolution of 1848, the German lower and middle classes joined forces to overthrow the autocratic elite running the country, and lost. Rather than stick around and await the one-percenters to ash cigars on their heads, the proletariat packed their lederhosen and hopped aboard the next ship to America. Here, most of the freedoms they'd fought for already awaited them, such as democracy and freedom of the press. One immigrant wrote:

> *The rich stand on the same footing as the poor . . . no*
> *German ought to be ashamed to pursue any occupation . . .*
> *above all there are no princes or corrupt courts.*[3]

Many under Stalin's and Hitler's regimes, torn between two terrible moustaches, fled for our borders in the 1930s and 1940s. For them, the freedom from religious or political persecution was worth uprooting their lives and taking a chance in a foreign land.

One such immigrant, the son of a Jewish family in Germany, sensed bad tidings in the early 1930s and fled continental Europe to settle on the sunny shores of California. During Hitler's rise to power, he cautiously snuck back into Belgium only to learn the Nazis had confiscated his sailboat for no-Jews-allowed booze cruises. Worse, they later turned his home into a Hitler Youth camp. Righteously indignant, he renounced his German citizenship and continued his world-changing work within the freedom and safety of America's borders. His name was Albert Einstein, and he spent the rest of the war developing a bomb to drop on Nazi boat parties.

So for hundreds of years, the American Dream was the *possibility* of prosperity and success unhindered by artificial barriers put in place by reigning parties or classes. For most of the world looking from the outside in, that was good enough.

Over time, however, the American Dream developed into the actual *achievement* of prosperity. Observing the 1849 Gold Rush, historian H. W. Brands wrote:

> *The new dream . . . the dream of instant wealth . . . became a prominent part of the American psyche.*[4]

Historian James Truslow Adams acknowledged the growing role of material wealth in the American Dream in his 1931 book *Epic of America*:

> *The American Dream, that has lured tens of millions . . . has not been a dream of mere material plenty, though that has doubtlessly counted heavily. It has been much more than that. It has been a dream of being able to grow to the fullest development as man and woman . . .*[5]

Adams wasn't the only writer to address the prominence of materialism in the new American Dream. We all remember a short read from high school called *The Great Gatsby*, in which F. Scott Fitzgerald portrays the moral decay of the American Dream in the 1920s. After World War I, an era of unprecedented wealth shifted our mindset toward material excess and the empty pursuit of pleasures, allegorized by Gatsby's pursuit of Daisy. However, as Fitzgerald warns through his characters, this pursuit leads to moral bankruptcy (literally) and us floating face down in a pool (figuratively). Following Gatsby's death, our narrator, Nick, moves back to the Midwest to score some cheese curds and build a new life where the morality of the old American Dream still exists.

The new dream . . . the dream of instant wealth . . . became a prominent part of the American psyche.

Sadly, Fitzgerald only sold twenty-five thousand copies of *Gatsby* before his death in 1940, and few of our predecessors had the time or money during the Depression to pick up the 450-page *Epic of America*. So neither book could stymy the spreading influence of materialism with the new American Dream. Plus, by the end of World War II, a single idea would forever orient our nation's ethos toward capital gains over wholesome morals.

GDP: The International Expansion of the American Dream

After World War II, a world covered in ash became fertile breeding ground for fresh ideologies. The old world had collapsed, and rapidly industrialized nations like America and Russia had come out on top. But since Stalin was still heaving people into gulags, most nations turned to us as a thought leader. To create some order in the postwar economic landscape, we offered the world a concentrated dose of the American Dream.

In 1937, American economist Simon Kuznets proposed the gross domestic product (GDP) as an objective measure of each nation's wealth to the US Congress. The GDP was the monetary value of all goods and services produced by a country within a certain time period, a.k.a. what that country was worth to the rest of the world.

Toward the end of the war, as liberated nations licked their wounds and put out fires, the world's newest economic superpower proposed that we all begin measuring our GDPs, not unlike a bodybuilder proposing a pull-up contest in a hospital. During the Bretton Woods Conference of 1944, which established international financial institutions such as the World Bank and International Monetary Fund, the GDP became the agreed-upon standard for international wealth, with Uncle Sam flexing on top.

Basically, we created an international metric for success that we were already winning, and began reveling in our self-created capitalist Eden. This certainly wasn't a bad thing *yet*; after all, the increased wealth of young couples led to the baby boom, and our exploding advertising industry would eventually give us *Mad Men.*

Speaking of, television soon played a pivotal role in shaping the modern American Dream. In 1948, merely 0.4 percent of American households had a television. In just ten years that number rose to 83.2 percent.[6] Shows like *I Love Lucy* and *Leave It To Beaver*, along with advertisements in between, slowly gave rise to more tangible goals for middle-class America: a well-paying job involving a dapper hat and double-breasted suit, a car or two, and a house in the 'burbs. For many families, however, these weren't long-term aspirations. After all, many soldiers returning from war could afford to buy a car and put a down payment on a house without even stepping foot in an interview. The American Dream of the white picket fence and the Cadillac wasn't just an aspirational ethos; it was the week's shopping list.

To summarize, the wealth explosion in the 1920s taught us to make money to be happy. The media and advertising boom of the 1950s taught us *what to buy* to be happy. **In a century, the American Dream had evolved from a checklist of *freedoms* to a checklist of *things*.** Though plainly tainted by capitalism, the new American Dream received little literary condemnation, presumably because of its wide attainability and crowded finish line. After all, who could condemn a contest where most hardworking Americans were winners?

So let's fast-forward two generations to us. Sure, we're graduating into the aftermath of a recession, but the economy's slowly nursing itself back to health. Should the American Dream checklist still serve as an inspiration for us, or is it time for new life goals?

Well, let's look at our financial viability to achieve the American Dream. In 2016, the average debt load for a graduating college senior was $37,172.[7] Right off the bat, our American Dream scorecard reads -1 Cadillac.

At least we're making more when we graduate with our obscenely expensive degrees, right? Nope. Unemployment sits at approximately 8 percent for educated graduates, and when you eventually get a job, we're making less than $50,000 per year on average, or enough to cover the Starbucks we drank in college (or if you're in med school, this month). We're the first generation expected to make *less* than our parents out of college, whereas we graduate with astronomically more debt.[8]

Nowadays, achieving our parents' American Dream of the well-paying job, big suburban house, and shiny new wheels in the driveway is as realistic as winning NASCAR in a Prius.

So when 41 percent of the respondents to that survey I mentioned earlier called achieving the Dream "impossible," is that what they were referring to? Funny enough, that survey had no predefined American Dream. People were simply asked, "Do you think the American Dream has become impossible for most people to achieve?" This allowed folks to respond based upon their own definitions of the American Dream, which were not recorded.

So what *does* the American Dream mean to our generation? As with each generation before us, have we Millennials defined our own already?

Using Reddit, word of mouth, and even Tinder,[1] I asked as many Millennials as I could what their American Dream is. **Are society's overarching goals helping generate happy lives? Or is the American Dream just a bloated, media-perpetuated monster that we need to ceremoniously burn as all 84 million of us hold hands?**

The second most common answer was legalized weed, but the overwhelming majority of us report that our generation's American Dream is simply to live debt-free. In fact, according to a 2015

---

[1] Girls were amazingly responsive to this opener.

survey, a third of us would even sell our kidneys to get out of debt.[9]

How sad is that? **Our grandparents got a yacht-sized Buick with no seat belts and a big suburban house to hang war medals in, while we're a depressing ATM receipt away from listing our kidneys on Craigslist.**

Our American Dream, then, seems less like a patriotic charge toward prosperity and more like a cynical relegation to our fate. I'll get the kerosene.

But before I do, let's remember that the world is a messed-up place, and while America isn't perfect, it's a whole hell of a lot better than many alternatives. One hundred and fifty years ago, immigrants fostered a wholesome American Dream, one that surely instilled a fresh perspective and inspired more happiness-building life goals. What can we learn from migrant Millennials *today*?

The Changing Ethos of Immigrant Millennials

To find out, I spoke with a Kenyan scholar, a Siberian scientist, and a jovial Belizean who defied death in two countries. What does the American Dream mean to them? Can we use their driving life goals to create a new American Dream for ourselves?

Hurry Boy, It's Waiting There for You

When Mark was fourteen, his father unexpectedly picked him up from school to head to the American embassy in Nairobi. Once there, he was subject to a head-to-toe physical exam, x-rays, and interviews. "I had no idea what was going on."

Mark had just begun his first semester at Starehe Boys' Centre, one of the top high schools in Kenya. For him, this was a Herculean achievement. Kenyan students like Mark studied for the high school entrance exam, the Kenya Certificate of Primary Education (KCPE), throughout their childhoods. And like many others, Mark had gotten a leg up by attending boarding school to prepare for the exam in isolation from the distractions of a traditional home and social life. "There's not as much pressure to get a 2400 on the SSAT or SAT in America," he says. "If you want a future in Kenya, there's pressure to score a 500 on the KCPE."

The grueling, four-day exam tests math, English and Swahili, current systems of government, science, three religions, and more. Mark had scored a 357; not perfect, but enough to rank him near the top of his class and open doors to the best high schools in Kenya, including Starehe.

As he rode home from the embassy full of questions, his family finally broke the news: his stepmother had won a green card application through the American embassy's lottery system, and his entire family would soon be moving to America. Mark was thrilled; he'd grown to revere American culture through television, music, and reading *Animorphs* and *The Hardy Boys*. "I felt like things were just better there."

But something didn't add up. At the time, Kenya flourished unthreatened by neighboring unrest, and Mark had just gained entry to one of the country's finest educational institutions. So why had his stepmother secretly been entering the lottery system for years?

His parents' answer bewildered him: they sought better education for him and his siblings. Tension and incredulity spread among Mark's extended family, as they couldn't believe his parents would uproot him from a school he'd spent his childhood earning a place in. But once he took a critical look at his higher education, Mark started to understand his parents' decision.

After high school, Kenyan students take the Kenya Certificate of Secondary Education (KCSE): the KCPE's brutal bigger brother. The KCSE dwarfs the SAT in scope, covering a seemingly absurd swath of topics from Hinduism to aviation, biochemistry to computer science. Furthermore, where you score best on the KCSE essentially defines your college major and career prospects. **For many Kenyans, the results of this month-long exam dictate the rest of their lives.**

Thus, freedom of education became Mark's American Dream. During his family's bizarre flight odyssey from Nairobi to Dubai,

London, New York, then Atlanta, Mark fantasized about exploring a wide variety of subjects in American high school like a kid in a curricular candy shop. In America, he could study and work in a field driven by his passions, not assigned by his scores.

Mark received financial aid at an equally prestigious high school in Georgia and attended Duke University, where he chose to major in mechanical engineering. While he was skilled in math and science, he discovered a passion for teaching and is now training to become a math teacher at Columbus State University.

Sadly, his divergence from the lucrative career path of an engineer came with a cost. Three years after graduation, Mark suffers from limited financial wiggle room. He simply calls his new American Dream "freedom from financial worry." "Now I have to think about where I'm going to get money to afford the lifestyle I want to live," which includes traveling, an apartment, and simply paying his bills.

Once Mark graduated from our education system, he'd accomplished the American Dream he'd envisioned since leaving Nairobi. In a way, his American Dream was temporary; his *new* American Dream of simply making enough to maintain a modest lifestyle sadly rings of familiarity.

But what might a foreign Millennial who's a little further along in their career path feel about the Stars and Stripes? What does the American Dream mean to a Millennial who left behind a more complete life in another country?

The Russian Dream: Leave Russia

Despite being the size of Boulder, Colorado, Roman's hometown of Seversk didn't officially exist on any map until 1992. For decades it served as a Russian "secret city" where the Soviets hid nuclear weapons and research. When Roman and his parents left the city to visit relatives, they'd have to pass six military checkpoints to reenter. Roman withheld fine details of his hometown from me, including why his parents were living there, because "people related to power will not be happy to find this in your book," but did concede that he enjoyed his secret-city upbringing. Despite the bleak omnipresence of frosty barbed wire, living in Seversk proved advantageous. Military cities were better supplied than others, so Roman and his sister got to share a fresh apple every day for dessert.

When he was ten, Roman's unforgettable biology teacher, Ms. Yapparova, saw promise in him and began tutoring him after school. Soon, Roman devoted his whole life to studying biology. Within a few years, he was dominating youth Biology Olympiads and entered college early, studying biochemistry at Siberian State Medical University while simultaneously performing research in a cardiology lab—all before his seventeenth birthday.

After graduation, Roman moved to Novosibirsk, the third-largest city in Russia and first largest you've never heard of. As he began studying HIV-1 vaccines, the reality of life as a Russian scientist set in with the comforting warmth and hope of a Russian winter.

"Scientists in the United States are part of middle class. In Russia, majority of scientists are poor people." The disappointments didn't end at the proletariat paycheck. In America, lab results could arrive in as little as two days. In Russia, they could take up to six months to show up, if at all. To make things worse, shifty government agencies routinely shuffled around his grant money, preventing him from forecasting his finances.

Fed up, Roman began planning a move to America. His American Dream was to enjoy the higher living standards and research freedoms of an American scientist. "You know, less bulls***."

In 2009, Roman moved to Arizona, a place famous for having zero Russian winters. After he'd settled, he "couldn't sleep for a month . . . I could not stop feeling euphoria." Best of all, he no longer had to share fruit with his sister. "Could you imagine when I got access to all fruits in the United States and had enough money to buy it?" During his first month in America, Roman spent slightly more on fruit than he did on rent.

Returning to the American Dream, Roman thrives in the freedoms our borders provide every day. A fervent outdoorsman, he loves exploring a country where more often than not he can step outside and still feel his face. "I have huge opportunities. Just imagine how many people want to visit the Grand Canyon; millions never will." But he still asserts that his initial infatuation with America was short-lived. Soon, "everything was familiar and I never felt the same euphoria again."

So for both Mark and Roman, their American Dreams served as temporary honeymoons, failing to evolve into lifelong, wholesome goals or clear guidelines for further happiness. While they've certainly improved their baseline happiness levels by moving here, both have settled into the rat race just like you and me, scavenging for happiness along the way.

Still, their backgrounds had something in common. They left behind stable, if not optimal, lives in their old countries to seek an upgrade. What might be the attitude of a Millennial who came here under more extreme circumstances?

Geez Belize

The tropical paradise of Belize ranks today as one of the happiest countries in the world, but as Julian grew up in the 1990s, the Caribbean hamlet served as a transit hub for cocaine shipments, festering from corruption, famine, and neglect from international Samaritans. Its tiny population of 238,000 eked out an existence in a cauldron of violence, and at the age of ten, Julian's childhood ended in an instant.

As he carried a box of chickens alongside a busy highway to his grandmother's, Julian heard the sound of revving engines and squealing tires approaching him from behind. *That* awful sound was instantly familiar, but the accompanying staccato of strange pops wasn't. The ferocious cacophony caught up to him as two motorcycle gangs rocketed past, wildly firing automatic weapons at each other. The deafening sound caused Julian to flee from the road. But as they tore past, Julian dropped the chickens and clutched his stomach. Blood seeped through his fingers as he rocked over and screamed for help.

The local doctors were able to extract the bullet and save his life, but to prevent complications he would need kidney surgery in a more developed country. Through some bribery and forged paperwork, Julian's family was able to move him to America where he received the operation he needed. He'd live with his grandfather in Los Angeles, but he'd quickly learn that sewing someone up and releasing them in South Central is like excusing someone from rehab and releasing them at Bonnaroo; he wouldn't stand a chance.

Sure enough, as he walked home from school one day, he unknowingly passed within a few feet of a drug deal about to go sour. After a short verbal altercation, one man brandished an assault rifle and began indiscriminately firing in Julian's direction. Hearing the now-familiar pop of gunshots again, he dove for safety. "Palm trees make really solid cover from gunfire," he told me fifteen years later, without looking up from his sandwich.

Julian spent the next eight years rotating through foster homes and abusive family households. His grandfather once slammed his head in a doorway for leaving crumbs on the toaster. His aunt and uncle wouldn't share food with him. But he'd never report them out of fear that legal intervention would lead to someone scrutinizing his shifty paperwork and deporting him.

At this point, he said, his overarching life goal was to survive. More specifically, his American Dream was to live a life of safety, autonomy, and freedom. He knew Los Angeles wasn't the real America he'd dreamed about.

So for years, Julian kept his head down and studied, telling his college counselor, "Get me far away from here."

In 2009 he began attending college on the East Coast, where he says he finally achieved his American Dream. "Every day was a celebration of life and safety." He had food, shelter, and the freedom to explore his life options.

So when I spoke with him in 2015, was he still satisfied with his achievement? No; in fact, he says, his definition of the American Dream had changed, quickly and drastically.

After the first semester of his freshman year, the euphoria of his newfound predicament had worn off and left a hangover. In college, Julian became bored, directionless, and even depressed. "My old goal was don't get shot. My new goal ... well, I didn't have one." Julian found the achievement of his old American Dream unfulfilling, and sought a new one in its place.

Over time, the ingredients of the modern American Dream began to assimilate in front of him. He soaked in advertising through sporting events and a casual TV addiction. He began noticing when his friends bought nicer things, and as an engineer, he took interest in how lucrative his opportunities could be. Eventually, he decided on a goal and stuck with it. "Y'all are here to get those fancy lives for yourselves," he remembers thinking. "All the cool kids are doing it, so I'll do it, too!"

At graduation, he recalls only half-kiddingly thinking, *Let's all go out and get that picket fence!* **Sadly, reality immediately slapped down his aspirations with an icy brutality.** After Julian walked across the stage and shook the chancellor's hand, he opened his diploma cover to find not a record of his accomplishment, but a bill stating how much he still owed the university—a big one. Julian saw his white picket fence slip away before even throwing his graduation cap.

Even after arriving in America, Julian maintained the antiquated American Dream of achieving safety. Mark and Roman valued freedom. But once all three had achieved their early life goals, their American Dreams, they settled into a familiar melancholy. No fresh ideals aligned them toward lifelong happiness. Julian had *tried* adopting the modern American Dream, and it immediately bit him in the ass.

So today's American Dream is at best the depressing aspiration to live debt-free and at worst a disheartening illusion. Either way, one thing is clear: we need a new one. We need a new ethos, a new generational mindset, which drives us to achieve a higher level of life satisfaction and happiness.

Perhaps like we've done with pop singers and pizza, we should just borrow one from another country.

The Scandinavian Dream:
Why "Swedish Chef" Is Visibly the Happiest Muppet

Maybe we should be calling the American Dream the Scandinavian Dream.

—Economist Joseph Stiglitz

Let's look back at the United Nations World Happiness rankings I mentioned earlier. If we didn't win, who did, and why?

Year after year, the happiest countries in the world are all found in Northern Europe. Switzerland, Iceland, Denmark, and Norway make up the top four, respectively, walloping us in three categories. And no, they aren't black metal, chocolate, and yodeling.

The first category is simple: longer life expectancy. Northern Europeans simply take better care of themselves, are a bit healthier, and are thus happier.

The second gets more interesting. National generosity was deemed so strongly indicative of national happiness that it's weighted equally to GDP in the overall calculation. Researchers collected generosity figures by measuring not how *much* was donated, but *how many* people donated across all income levels.

Lastly, Scandinavian countries beat our pants off in the category of social support. When things get tough, people in these countries feel that they always have somebody to count on, whether it's a relative, friend, or neighbor.

Some psychologists believe this sense of national community stems from a social code unique to these four countries called the Law of Jante. The Law comprises ten social "commandments" collectively interpreted as "don't think you're better than anyone else." Scandinavians de-emphasize self-promotion and individual success in favor of collective well-being. Before you cry communism, the Law of Jante isn't about closing the wealth gap at the barrel of a gun. Rather, it's about humility, empathy, and living within your means to create a more egalitarian society.

Scandinavians get rich sometimes, but it's rarely their driving priority, and they generally don't flaunt their wealth. The founder of IKEA, a Swede by the name of Ingvar Kamprad, famously drove a 1993 Volvo 240 until it was no longer roadworthy. By contrast, American entrepreneur Robert Herjavec from the ABC show *Shark Tank* drives a $500,000 Lamborghini convertible, an obscene display of opulence we could've looked past until he drove it up to *four other supercars and a private jet* in the show's introduction.

With regards to fame, everybody knows who Mark Zuckerberg is—even a Japanese sushi chef, which I cleverly inferred when she blurted, "You look like a sexy Mark Zuckerberg! Thanks for make the Facebook!" But do you know who Niklas Zennström is? How about Daniel Ek? They invented Skype and Spotify, respectively. In fact, Mr. Ek's Wikipedia page is so unostentatious, it's shorter than the page for Gaylord Silly, a French long-distance runner and tree surgeon. The happiest people on earth, then, don't seem to bother with the limelight.

Outside of work, Scandinavians' social support spills into home life as well. Many Northern Europeans live in cohousing communities: large, dorm-style buildings where residents live in conjoined private homes but share communal spaces such as playgrounds, kitchens, childcare facilities, gyms, and home offices. Residents prepare meals and eat together, garden together, and generally support each other on a daily basis. While cohousing communities save residents plenty of time and money, they weren't conceived with these benefits in mind. Rather, the Danes created them in the 1960s to cure loneliness and strengthen the social fabric of the nation.

Many Scandinavian college grads move into cohousing communities to continue reaping the benefits of living in a dorm-style social community. "I think this kind of living arrangement is fantastic," says Rikke, a twenty-six-year-old Danish grad student. "There's always someone to hang out with, and if I'm in the mood to be alone, I can just go to my room."[II]

[II] Interested in living in a cohousing community? There are over 160 of them in American now. Visit cohousing.org.

So while we surge ahead in GDP, countries of Northern Europe consistently have us beat in personal health, generosity, and social support. But they also hold a secret weapon within their borders: a foundation for lifelong happiness that we in America lack.

Maslow's Hierarchy of Needs: The Layers of a Happy Life

Scandinavian countries will be happier than us for the foreseeable future, and their secret lies within a seventy-year-old technicolor pyramid. In his 1943 paper "A Theory of Human Motivation," psychologist Abraham Maslow summarized the general order of needs we're instinctually driven to fill before realizing our fullest potential. First, we seek the basics like clothing, shelter, and food. Then, we aspire to long-term health and safety. Once we've taken care of those, we pursue a basic feeling of belonging and acceptance in society. Our penultimate goal is to build confidence and command the respect of our peers. Finally, we seek wisdom and a deeper feeling of purpose through creativity, passion, and achieving our dreams.

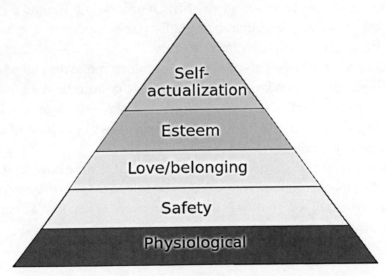

Maslow's Hierarchy of Needs[10]

In essence, we can't achieve higher fulfillment (and our happiness potential) without first fulfilling our most basic needs. On a global scale, there's a direct correlation between a country's national happiness and its ability to provide basic needs for its citizens.

In America, many people struggle to build happy, fully realized lives because they're too busy trying to fulfill their most basic needs. And that goes beyond material wealth; even at the top of the socioeconomic food chain, our wealthiest denizens commonly suffer from a lack of love and belonging.

By contrast, Norway, Denmark, Switzerland, and Iceland all provide free education and healthcare for life to all their citizens. Unhindered by student debt or eye-popping medical bills, Scandinavians enjoy a more stable, less stressful existence. Combined with their stronger social-support system, Northern Europeans are essentially *born* on level three of Maslow's pyramid, with a huge head start on happiness.

The tradeoff they pay, of course, is being taxed out the wazoo. Scandinavians pay as much as 57 percent of their income in taxes to cover the cost of their silky social safety net. Consumer goods are expensive as well; when released in Denmark, the iPhone 6 cost $1,000. However, Scandinavians gladly pay this price in exchange for significantly lower national anxiety.

So despite the popularity of satanic black metal and a lack of sunlight, **Scandinavians are the happiest people in the world, while we're the richest. As they laugh and play with locally made Legos in their cohousing communal spaces, we cry alone in our big, empty houses and BMWs.**

Clearly, this disparity means a nation's GDP may have little to do with its overall happiness. But to be fair, we never *told* the rest of the world that cash flow is the best measure of a nation's overall welfare.

Did we?

A Worldwide Motion toward Happiness

Let's leave the land of Vikings and Legos and turn our attention back on ourselves for a bit, because Scandinavian-style socialized democracy isn't the on/off switch to national happiness. After all, we have deeper problems woven into our social fabric that lend to our slipping happiness levels. To earn the greatest GDP of the top-fifteen happiest countries, we work on average forty-seven hours per week and give up our vacation; we're the *only* developed country that doesn't guarantee a single paid-vacation day or holiday.[11] By contrast, the Germans have thirty-four. We also place less value on our health. Thirty-two percent of Americans are obese, compared to less than four percent of the Japanese.[12]

As a result of our workaholic nature, we've become a cautionary tale to the rest of the world of how GDP doesn't measure happiness. But this notion is far from new. As early as 1959, economist Moses Abramovitz doubted GDP was a meaningful metric for a nation's welfare.

We must be highly skeptical of the view that long-term changes in the rate of growth of welfare can be gauged even roughly from changes in the rate of growth of output.[13]

Rapper Notorious B.I.G. frames it another way:

Mo' money mo' problems.

Unfortunately, Biggie wasn't around in 1962 when JFK's economic advisors coined Okun's law, which states that for every three-point rise in GDP, unemployment will fall one percentage point. Fewer jobless citizens means more nationwide happiness, right? The logic seemed infallible, so Okun's law solidified GDP as our national welfare metric for the rest of the twentieth century.

As we simultaneously dropped bombs on Vietnam and acid at Woodstock, other nations grew skeptical that America was growing true happiness. In 1972, the king of Bhutan, a mystical mountain kingdom wedged between China and India, declared his nation would begin measuring Gross National Happiness to guide public policies. In 1990, the United Nations launched the Human Development Index to create, in the words of UN economist Mahbub ul Haq, "an index as vulgar as the GDP but more relevant to our own lives."[14]

But in true American fashion, we stuck to our guns. In 1999, the US Department of Commerce declared the GDP to be one of the greatest inventions of the twentieth century. Following the 9/11 attacks and the tech-bubble burst, when the international market took a nosedive, the codependent economies of the world watched as our capitalist empire shook at its foundations. *Will it fall?* Not yet. By 2006 the shaking had stopped, and we appeared as strong as ever.

After 9/11, however, keen-eyed economists around the world noticed new cracks in our system, notably an embarrassing fallacy in our GDP-equals-welfare logic. From 2001 to 2006, our GDP continued to *rise* while the personal incomes of Americans *fell*. But before bigger questions could be raised, the greatest crack of all brought the entire system crashing down. The 2008 housing crisis exposed an institution built upon deplorable greed, widespread corruption, and moral bankruptcy. Seeing the fires on Wall Street and millions of despondent, devastated Americans, our economic allies were done assuming that the pursuit of wealth would eventually lead to happiness. **In 2008, the world had seen enough of the American Dream.**

British Prime Minister David Cameron was among the first to take action. "It's time we admitted that there's more to life than money . . . Wellbeing can't be measured by money or traded in markets. It's about the beauty of our surroundings, the quality of our culture, and, above all, the strength of our relationships . . . It's time we focused not just on GDP but on GWB—general wellbeing."[15]

By 2010, the British government had begun surveying national happiness alongside traditional economic metrics. Less than a year later, the UN General Assembly passed a measure encouraging nations to begin measuring their citizens' happiness and using that, rather than GDP, to influence public-policy decisions.

Learning from our lesson, America has begun moving in that direction as well. While our federal government is understandably busy with other to-dos, like fighting ISIS and keeping Billy Bush off of the White House lawn, well-being research has blossomed at the state level. In 2015, Vermont, Oregon, Colorado, Hawaii, and Maryland began adopting a replacement for GDP called the genuine progress indicator, which wraps happiness into twenty-six measures of the state's overall welfare, including cost of lost leisure time and value of volunteer work. By the time you read this, more states will hopefully have adopted this model!

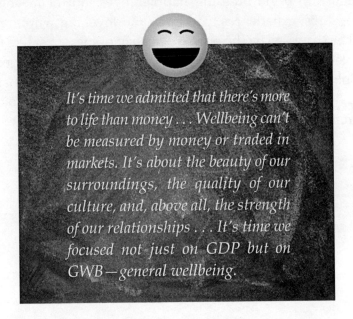

It's time we admitted that there's more to life than money . . . Wellbeing can't be measured by money or traded in markets. It's about the beauty of our surroundings, the quality of our culture, and, above all, the strength of our relationships . . . It's time we focused not just on GDP but on GWB—general wellbeing.

Also, before we move on, I want to acknowledge that while I may have seemed to roast America pretty hard in parts of this chapter, I, like Mark, Roman, and Julian, am extremely grateful to live here. We're not a perfect nation, but how could we be with such unprecedented diversity and freedom of expression? In short, I doubt this book could have been easier to write in any other country.

To summarize, the world has always searched for the roots of happiness and satisfaction, but our attempts thus far have been misguided. In the ashes of World War I, our predecessors turned toward power and imperialism. In the ashes of World War II, recovering nations turned toward capitalism. Now, in the ashes of the global financial crisis, nations are finally cutting through the BS and exploring true happiness.

So our generation's cloudy economic predicament has a silver lining: it's helped spur the world into centering public policies around happiness. Despite what the media would have you believe, the world is entering a happiness renaissance.

But why don't you and I get a head start right now? In the following pages, we'll dive into the most studied and proven techniques to begin building happier lives, full of meaningful relationships, experiences, passions, and love. Big words, right? You'll be surprised by the power of true happiness, just like I was.

So let's get into the meat and potatoes of modern positive psychology and start laying out some lifestyle changes for happier living. We'll begin with a term I've peppered throughout the beginning of the book: what exactly is "true happiness"?

References:

1) Helliwell, John F., Richard Layard, and Jeffrey Sachs, eds. *World Happiness Report 2016 Update*. New York: Sustainable Development Solutions Network, 2016.

2) Henderson, Ben. "American Dream Slipping Away, but Hope Intact." August 13, 2013. Accessed September 19, 2015. https://today.yougov.com/news/2013/08/07/american -dream-slipping-away-hard-work-still-count/.

3) Bogen, F. W., *The German in America* (Boston, 1851), quoted in Stephen Ozment, *A Mighty Fortress: A New History of the German People* (New York: Harper Perennial, 2004), 170–71.

4) Brands, H. W. and H. W. Br. *The Age of Gold: The California Gold Rush and the New American Dream*. New York: Bantam Doubleday Dell Publishing Group, 2002.

5) Adams, James Truslow, M. J. Gallagher, and illustrated by M. J. Gallagher. *The Epic of America*. 2nd ed. United States: Greenwood Press, 1980.

6) Baughman, James L. "Television Comes to America, 1947-57." March 1993. Accessed December 29, 2015. http://www.lib.niu.edu/1993/ihy930341.html.

7) Josuweit, Andy. "U.S. Student Loan Debt Statistics for 2016." Accessed September 19, 2016. https://studentloanhero.com/student-loan-debt-statistics/.

8) Carrick, Rob. "Gen-Y's Pain Is Real: Paycheques Tell the Tale." November 28, 2013. Accessed October 16, 2016. http://www.theglobeandmail.com/globe- investor/personal-finance/household-finances/gen-y- wages-the-pain-is-real/article15638656/.

9) Zhen, Simon. "How Far Would You Go to Get Rid of Your Student Debt? [Infographic]." October 23, 2015. Accessed February 19, 2016.

https://www.mybanktracker.com/news/how-far-would-you-go-get-rid-your-student-debt-infographic.

10) Drinnien, Beverly A., Donald B. Irwin, and Janet A. Simons. "MASLOW'S HIERARCHY OF NEEDS." 1987. Accessed January 5, 2016.
https://web.archive.org/web/20100211014419/http://honolulu.hawaii.edu/intranet/committees/FacDevCom/guidebk/teachtip/maslow.htm.

11) Saad, Lydia. "The '40-Hour' Workweek Is Actually Longer -- by Seven Hours." August 29, 2014. Accessed May 16, 2016.
http://www.gallup.com/poll/175286/hour-workweek-actually-longer-seven-hours.aspx.

12) Senauer, Benjamin and Masahiko Gemma. "Why Is the Obesity Rate So Low in Japan and So High in The U.S.? Some Possible Economic Explanations." February 2, 2006. Accessed December 29, 2015.
https://ideas.repec.org/p/ags/umrfwp/14321.html.

13) Abramovitz, Moses. *The Allocation of Economic Resources: Essays in Honor of Bernard Francis Haley*. United States: Stanford University Press, 1966.

14) Dickinson, Elizabeth. "GDP: A Brief History." January 3, 2011. Accessed January 10, 2016.
http://foreignpolicy.com/2011/01/03/gdp-a-brief-history/.

15) Stratton, Allegra. "David Cameron Aims to Make Happiness the New GDP." *The Guardian* (The Guardian), November 14, 2010.
https://www.theguardian.com/politics/2010/nov/14/david-cameron-wellbeing-inquiry.

Chapter 1 Takeaways:

- The seeds to a happy life aren't naturally sewn into American culture. Adaptation and media propagation drive us toward goals that don't create true happiness.
- The happiest countries in the world focus on humility, health, and social connectedness.
- A worldwide movement has begun to measure national happiness and well-being instead of GDP, and use the former to guide public-policy decisions.

Coming Up in Chapter 2:

- The most surreal night of my life occurs at a secret sweat-lodge gathering
- Set point theory creates a thirty-year dark age of positive psychology
- A happiness revolution begins behind the Berlin Wall

Chapter 2
The Meaning of True Happiness

We are always getting ready to live but never living.
—Ralph Waldo Emerson

Aristotle concluded 2,300 years ago that as humans, we all seek happiness. We search out power, money, beauty, and other things simply because we believe that they'll make us happier. While they all *can*, the amount and longevity of the happiness these things provide vary greatly. As a result, to this day humans still head in wildly different directions in search of the same thing: a happy and fulfilling life.

Perhaps it's this plethora of avenues that prevents people from training us how to be happy. They train us how to be rich, or educated, or have more sex, but they never cut through the bull straight to the bottom line. In this book, I aim to do exactly that.

So how, as a twenty-six-year-old, have I accrued the knowledge to write and speak with even a modicum of confidence on the subject? Well, not many people quit their jobs to study happiness full time. More people probably quit their jobs to chase Bigfoot.

In my journeys, I've found that learning true happiness is like learning a language in a new country. I had picked up a few things on my own growing up, but for most of my life, fluency eluded me. Without a deeper understanding of the ingredients of a happy life, I was destined to live well below my happiness potential. To reiterate my philosophies from the intro, I'd probably stumble upon a source or two of true happiness *eventually*, but I wasn't satisfied with that solution. I wanted to explore *all* of them, first to save myself from the throes of depression, then to help my friends, family, and everyone else who would listen.

To understand true happiness, I surrounded myself with textbooks, teachers, experiences, and fellow students, becoming fully immersed in the language. During my fast track to happiness, I lived in multiple temples and monasteries, bungee-jumped over the Yangtze River, high-fived a Chinese millionaire, built a house with Buddhist monks, danced with Danes, and partied with Polynesians.

But perhaps my most enlightening happiness classroom was closer to home. For me, the meaning of true, lasting happiness *finally* came together on a frosty December evening, when I swallowed my reservations and followed a fellow student of happiness to a mysterious sweat lodge in East Atlanta.

A Yes-Man's Sweaty Test

"It's down this way, I think," Hill told me, less than reassuringly. Then he disappeared down a steep, pitch-black hill, his orange, chest-length hair bouncing under his purple pork-pie hat. The smell of sage overpowered me as I helplessly looked on into the darkness. I curled my toes into my flip-flops for better grip and a trivial amount of warmth. The ridiculousness of the situation struck me like a gong. *What am I doing here?*

Earlier that day, I had run into my mysterious, bohemian stepcousin, Hill, outside of a Smoothie King, and we caught up. Pleasantries gave way to a more meaningful discussion as I learned he had been working to publish a children's book on mindfulness called *Blue: A Mindfulness Tale*. He'd even gotten an illustrator from the TV show *Archer* to bring his characters to life. That evening I treated us to dinner and accepted a homemade hat pin as payment. Hill, nervous about his ongoing Kickstarter campaign to raise money for the book, concluded, "If you wanna blow off some stress, I'm heading to the sweat lodge tonight. Come with!"

Fast forward to later that evening, and Hill and I were blindly navigating a land trust in East Atlanta. Since we'd left our phones in the car, we had no light source other than a half moon to find the secret gathering. "Follow the scent of the sage," he cheeringly told me, his flip-flops flopping down the dark hill.

His advice sounded like the hippie equivalent of a hillbilly's famous last words: "Hold my beer."

Ahead of us, plastered against an otherwise thick, hilly Georgian forest, was a white fence with a blue towel spanning the only gap. Under the towel I could see teacup candles and hear the crackle of a wood fire. The scent of sage was palpable.

We crossed the threshold of the blue towel and entered what I can best describe as the inside of a meditator's mind. Candles and incense burned in a dozen places, providing an ominous glow against the looming, leafless dogwoods. To my right was an earthy hut resembling the modest home of a working-class hobbit, complete with an adorably sized door. Plastic mats splayed out to our left, while a wooden table sat to our right holding a jug of water, a few jars, and, of course, plenty of spare sage.

Reaching to light a teacup candle was an African American man in his midsixties, with two-tone dreadlocks dancing down to the small of his back. He turned to greet us with a warm, genuine smile.

"Welcome, my brothers." He introduced himself as Robert, though carried a tone as if he'd known us for years. "Allow me to bless you."

Hill took off his shirt and flip-flops, so I swiftly followed suit. Robert retrieved a palm-sized, handmade-looking bowl filled with burning sage. We stood with our arms out and legs apart as Robert began following the outline of our bodies, covering us in smoke.

"As always, we like to give thanks to the four elements. We salute the air, the fire, the water, and space." He then gestured to the sweat lodge. "We declare this a sacred space."

I resisted a cough as the incense filled my lungs. Having amply sage'd us, Robert retrieved a pot of clay. He spoke as he marked the center of our foreheads.

"With this, I declare you one of us and one with the Earth." He then embraced me in a tight hug. "Thanks for coming, brother."

Robert's sincerity cut through me like a hot knife through facetious butter. As he embraced me, my cynical preconceptions about the evening started to melt away.

About a dozen other attendees trickled in over the next few minutes. I was the only male without a beard or a tattoo. Most of the women stripped naked. I don't think I'd ever shaken hands with a nude woman before. I wondered when this would ever happen outside of a sweat-lodge situation. Maybe at a porn shoot.

Pure thoughts, Chris. Focus.

As soon as Robert had sufficiently sage'd everybody, he held open the hobbit door and we filed into the sweat lodge. To our left was a wood-burning stove, with a midnight-black pipe extending outward along the wall. Two levels of wooden benches surrounded the stove like a tiny amphitheater. We took our seats and Robert closed the door. Hill gently pounded my knee with his fist, signaling, *Are you digging this?* I wasn't sure yet— I'd only been in the questionable hippie oven for a few seconds.

The evening consisted of six twenty-minute segments, where we'd spend eight minutes in the lodge and twelve minutes outside to cool off and hydrate. As we exited the lodge, our sweat steamed off of our bodies until everyone appeared to be smoking like the Human Torch. While inside the lodge, Robert would lead us in a mindfulness activity.

"This time, we're going to say NO over and over to remind ourselves that we always have a choice. Say it with me, my brothers and sisters."

I muttered *NO*, but the sweat veterans were much louder. On the next *NO*, I joined the ferocity. It felt pretty good. We don't get many chances in everyday life to scream *NO* at the top of our lungs, unless we hear the in-flight movie is *Fifty Shades of Grey*.

We followed the *NO*s with a set of *YES*es and then *WOW*s. "Now, my brothers and sisters, we're going to share something we're currently passionate about."

A guy named Nikolai was learning Native American chants, and shared one with us. Jenni behind me had just opened an art gallery. The girl to my right, whose name I forgot, shared that she'd begun painting with her menstrual blood.

Holy f***! That's some next-level Lena Dunham s***! Deep breath . . . freeing my mind of judgment . . .

I shared how I was writing a book to help young people build happy lives. The woman next to me squeezed my knee and said, "Ashe, ashe" (an African expression akin to "right on"). The room echoed a few *ashe*s. Felt good, man.

Despite a few distractions from mindfulness, I thoroughly enjoyed the evening. I'd call the combination of camaraderie, heat, and meditation intoxicating, but *de*toxifying is a better descriptor. I truly felt as if I had let distractions and inner demons evaporate with the sweat and sage.

As we concluded the final session and filed out, Robert had us circle up and asked us whether we had hugged twelve people that day. A few chuckles emanated from the group, but Robert remained austere.

"My brothers and sisters, you are *hug deficient*! Please don't leave tonight until you've hugged twelve of each other. Ashe, and go in peace."

I first embraced Hill and thanked him for bringing me. Then Jerome, a chef, then Kelly, a substitute teacher. I also hugged Menstrual Monet. All of us hugged everyone else with a lengthy, meaningful squeeze usually reserved for tearful departures or survivors of *Die Hard*-style terrorist takeovers. **One woman nearly cried as she embraced me for ten seconds. What would've been a painfully awkward real-life situation actually felt sweet and liberating.**

Needless to say, it was an evening I'll never forget. I've since returned to the secretive sweat sessions with friends to share in the experience. Soon, Robert even began trusting me to "bless" the attendees with sage as he tended to the candlelighting. Nervous, I struggled to remember the four elements: *Earth, Wind, Fire, Heart?*

No, that's Captain Planet . . . Each time I blessed a new person and applied the clay to their forehead, I fought the burning temptation to say, "Simba."

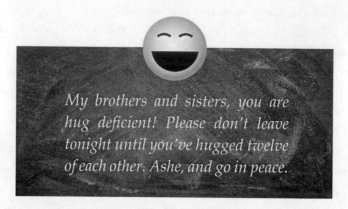

My brothers and sisters, you are hug deficient! Please don't leave tonight until you've hugged twelve of each other. Ashe, and go in peace.

I chose to bring up my sweat-lodge adventure here to illustrate how a single evening had brought me true, long-lasting happiness. My alternative that evening was to stay home indulging in kettle corn and Netflix, but instead I sought out an experience that involved meaningful social connection, personal growth, physical exertion, and novelty. I not only had a blast and felt happy in the moment, I actually raised my baseline happiness ever-so-slightly. Staying at home to binge-watch *Archer* as I filled a Snuggie with farts would've only provided short-term pleasure. After the sweat-lodge adventure, I woke up the next day, and the day after that, a little bit happier.

You don't need a sweat lodge and a gaggle of half-naked hippies to build true happiness; you just need to invest a little effort in the right places. But what exactly *is* this "true happiness"? Why does it have a lasting effect while our happiness from pleasures like Coke always dissipates?

The answer lies in how each affects our aforementioned baseline happiness, also known as our hedonic set points, or HSP. Set point theory is one of the earliest theories in modern happiness research, but, ironically, actually *stunted* further research for decades. For the Lewis and Clark of happiness, who set out to explore the far reaches of our happiness potential, set point theory was like discovering an impassable wall in the first fifty feet.

The History of Modern Happiness

In 1971, psychologists Philip Brickman and Donald Campbell coined the term "hedonic set point" to describe the average levels of happiness we feel every day, i.e., our baseline happiness.[1] They theorized that like our moods, temperament, and energy, our happiness can experience wild fluctuations, but these highs and lows are only temporary and we'll eventually return to our baselines.

Though set point theory was just that, a theory, a famous study conducted later in the decade layered evidence on the idea. In 1978, researchers followed both lottery winners and accident victims who'd suffered a permanent handicap. They found that within a year, both groups had returned to their previous, or baseline, levels of happiness.[2] If *those* two extremes couldn't change their long-term happiness, it's unlikely that anybody could.

As a result, set point theory became the dominant paradigm theory of happiness. So for years, many psychologists believed that our hedonic set points were genetically predetermined, and throughout our lives we could only experience minor variations of a few percentage points.

So the groovy, bell-bottomed psychologists of the 1970s believed with confidence that our long-term happiness was entirely out of our control, rendering further happiness research pretty pointless. In response to this bleak news, our parents desperately quested for happiness by dropping acid and listening to ABBA. *The horror . . .*

Thankfully, doubters emerged during this dark age of positive psychology. Into the 1980s and 1990s, psychologists continued trying to crack set point theory, but unfortunately, things got worse before they got better. In 1989, an eight-year study of life satisfaction failed to correlate extroversion and openness to new experiences with an increased frequency of positive life events.[3] In 1996, a longitudinal study of identical twins concluded that "trying to be happier may be as futile as trying to be taller," which sounds like the authors mixed in lyrics from their debut goth album.[4]

Set point theory, then, was positive psychology's equivalent to "the world is flat"—a widely accepted theory, loosely supported by inferential conclusions, in desperate need of some contradiction. So in 2002, positive psychologists formed a "Justice League" of happiness, convening at the First Annual International Positive Psychology Summit in Washington, DC. Their mission? Reignite happiness research and smash set point theory.

After the summit, researchers began chiseling away at set point theory with more hopeful conclusions. A 2004 study concluded, "Desirable outcomes, even economic ones, are often caused by well-being rather than the other way around."[5] A 2007 study correlated the character traits hope, love, curiosity, and zest with increased overall life satisfaction.[6]

But as American psychologists chiseled away at set point theory, the Germans showed up with a sledgehammer. In 2008 they released a study concluding "a direct test of set point theory shows it to be flawed." Their "test" was collecting and analyzing the reported happiness levels of sixty thousand German citizens over twenty-five years, since before the fall of the Berlin Wall. The authors concluded, "Results showing that long-term happiness can be substantially affected by individual choices are good news, not only for economists but also for governments and humankind."[7] In other words, the positive psychology Rebel Alliance had finally destroyed the set point theory Death Star.

However, this epic victory for happiness left us with a cliffhanger ending. What exactly *are* the "individual choices" leading to increased happiness over time? What were those Germans doing to raise their happiness over twenty-five years? Baking weed into their schnitzel? The authors of the study lacked the qualitative data to say for sure, but they postulated nonetheless; surely it had something to do with a lifetime of learning, social connectedness, and passions.

Still, the Germans had done game-changing work. Unshackled by set point theory, positive psychologists entered a renaissance of happiness research, rushing to discover the secrets behind long-term happiness, henceforth known as "authentic" or "true" happiness. The rest of this book, combined with Volume II, is a guide to everything they've found thus far. **Our young lives are a blank canvas on which to paint our futures. We're going to discuss the colors and strokes for creating a vibrant, successful, and happy life.** *Let me be your happiness Bob Ross.*

Now, as any good painter knows, the secret to a *lasting* masterpiece is a good layer of primer. In our case, we'll prime our lives for happiness with a few lifestyle adjustments. Let's start by reducing our reliance on pleasures.

Results showing that long-term happiness can be substantially affected by individual choices are good news, not only for economists but also for governments and humankind.

References:

1) Brickman, Philip, and Donald T. Campbell. "Hedonic relativism and planning the good society." *Adaptation-Level Theory* (1971): 287–305.

2) Brickman, Philip, Dan Coates, and Ronnie Janoff-Bulman. "Lottery winners and accident victims: Is happiness relative?" *Journal of Personality and Social Psychology* 36, no. 8 (1978): 917.

3) Headey, Bruce, and Alexander Wearing. "Personality, life events, and subjective well-being: toward a dynamic equilibrium model." *Journal of Personality and Social psychology* 57, no. 4 (1989): 731.

4) Lykken, David, and Auke Tellegen. "Happiness is a stochastic phenomenon." *Psychological Science* 7, no. 3 (1996): 186–189.

5) Diener, Ed, and Martin EP Seligman. "Beyond money toward an economy of well-being." *Psychological Science in the Public Interest* 5, no. 1 (2004): 1–31.

6) Peterson, Christopher, Willibald Ruch, Ursula Beermann, Nansook Park, and Martin EP Seligman. "Strengths of character, orientations to happiness, and life satisfaction." *The Journal of Positive Psychology* 2, no. 3 (2007): 149–156.

7) Headey, Bruce, Ruud Muffels, and Gert G. Wagner. "Long-running German panel survey shows that personal and economic choices, not just genes, matter for happiness." *Proceedings of the National Academy of Sciences* 107, no. 42 (2010): 17922–17926.

Chapter 2 Takeaways:

- Set point theory, the idea that our happiness is genetic and fluctuations are only temporary, stunted happiness research for decades.
- After measuring happiness levels over twenty-five years, in 2008 German researchers presented credible evidence that we can *build* happiness over time.
- Since their discovery, researchers have begun investigating and finding ways to increase our happiness for the long-term.

Coming Up in Chapter 3:

- Understanding pleasures, the nature of the happiness they provide, and how they can help or hurt our happiness
- A deeper look at our favorite pleasures
  - The exact percentage Facebook usage affects our happiness
  - How a military research secret redefined the processed-food industry
  - Finding the fulcrum where alcohol provides maximum happiness *and* pleasure
- How to avoid a life of pleasure addiction known as the "Rock Star Lifestyle"

Chapter 3
Say "Bon Voyage" to Pleasure Island

True happiness derives from a deep understanding of our suffering and of the workings of our mind. It isn't the happiness that we feel when we eat a bar of chocolate, enjoy the taste, and get a sugar high. These forms of happiness that most of us are acquainted with come and go quickly.
—Sister Dang Nhiem, *Mindfulness as Medicine*

All happiness derives from just two sources: true happiness and pleasure. The distinction is so important that the ancient Greeks avoided the umbrella term "happiness" altogether and used the words *hedonia* to loosely describe short-lived pleasure and *eudaimonia* to conversely describe meaningful, long-term happiness.[1]

While the true happiness we'll learn about in this book lasts and builds upon itself, pleasures provide short-lived spikes. A soda is the perfect example; sipping on a fizzy pop feels good while it lasts, but doesn't grow us as human beings. My friend Robbie is a die-hard Coke fanatic on the verge of declaring jihad on Pepsi, but even he doesn't fondly reminisce about a Coke he had in junior high, simply because the happiness it provided is long over. However, he and I both reminisce about our friends and favorite classes because those people and experiences had a lasting impact on our long-term happiness. Because of its temporary nature, pleasure often goes by another name: *fleeting happiness*.

Other examples of pleasures are TV, sex, food, drugs, shopping, and social media; all of these provide happiness "highs." But don't worry, **to build true happiness we don't need to purge pleasure from our lives and become the Amish Generation. Pleasures are part of a balanced happiness diet, providing a nice boost of bliss when we need it.**

For example, after a woeful day, we may just want to wrap ourselves in the warm embrace of Netflix and junk food. Similarly, when we're out with our friends on a Friday night, we may want to amplify the happiness of the evening with pleasures like toking a hookah or doing shots. My friend James is an avid socialite, but occasionally has "James Games" nights where he hermits in his apartment to marathon through the newest video games.

These occasional indulgences aren't a crime, nor will they ruin our true happiness. But problems arise when we *rely* on pleasures as our main source of happiness. Relying on pleasures to provide happiness is a dangerous pitfall, because when they lose their potency, we're not conditioned to rebalance our diet with true happiness. Instead, we often indulge in *more* pleasures, which destroys our wallets, minds, and bodies while our true happiness continues to atrophy.

If only I could think of an analogy our entire generation could identify with . . .

Pleasures: The Caffeine of Happiness

Let's compare our happiness to something more measurable on a daily basis: our energy. There are really just two ways to increase our energy: We can build our stamina by sleeping well and exercising, or boost ourselves temporarily using stimulants like caffeine or Adderall. Happiness works in a similar way; we can build our "happiness stamina" through social connection, learning, gratitude, meditation, etc., and feel naturally happier every day, or we can indulge in pleasures that boost our happiness temporarily.

A truly happy life, then, balances building our happiness stamina while occasionally indulging in pleasures for a pleasant kick. If we *only* drink caffeine and never sleep or exercise, we'll become weaker, and need progressively more caffeine to feel energized. Similarly, if we let our true happiness wilt, we'll become dependent on pleasures to feel happy again, which have a fast rate of diminishing returns. "We have to keep on having more food, more drugs or alcohol, more money, more sex, more things in order to feel pleasure," says Dr. Margaret Paul, author of *Inner Bonding*. "As a result, many people become addicted . . . needing more and more to feel a short-lived feeling of happiness."[2]

So if pleasures are expensive, short-lived, and unreliable, why do we love them so much? Well, for many of the same reasons we love coffee.

Pleasure Potency

First, pleasures are instantly gratifying. Sure, we could read a book and learn something meaningful, but the new season of *The Unbreakable Kimmy Schmidt* just came out on Netflix, and that show is *hilarious*.

A lot of our inclination toward pleasure is conditioned. We're born into an unequivocally pleasure-based society: Hollywood rakes in $100 billion/year,[3] while domestic fast-food chains make twice that.[4] When we were growing up, our parents were probably the best buffers to an all-pleasure diet, dictating healthy eating habits or dropping us off at summer camp for social growth.

But many of us don't internalize the value of these things in our youth; in fact, some people *never* internalize the value of lasting, often free, true happiness-based activities over expensive, fleeting pleasures. So they spend their lives buying and consuming, chasing that pleasure high while the meaningful parts of their existence waste away. Many one-percenters are so miserable, there's a new type of psychological counseling tailored just to them called "wealth therapy."

Second, pleasures are convenient. With vending machines, Netflix, the Internet, and fast food, pleasure is always within our reach. There's a highway exit I used to pass on my way back from college with two Waffle Houses—one for each direction of traffic. With a good arm, you could throw a waffle and hit the other one.

But nowhere is *hedonia* more ubiquitous than at college, a pleasure playground the likes of which we'd never experienced before in our teens. As freshmen, most of us were Charlies in Chocolate Factories, eyes widened before endless pleasures like drugs, video games, casual sex, and greasy food. The only thing stopping us was our underdeveloped sense of self-restraint.

As we progressed through college, most of us effectively balanced our pleasure intake with true happiness by joining clubs or groups, being social, studying abroad, and taking interesting classes. If we achieved this equilibrium between pleasure indulgence and true happiness-building in college, we probably had a good time.

As we entered the adult world, however, something happened to drive us toward pleasure again. Due to the demands of work or grad school, we began to feel more *tired* all the time. Not *physically* exhausted, as if we'd just left the gym, but *mentally* exhausted. There's a term for this; it's called ego depletion, or the idea that each day we draw upon a limited amount of mental energy and willpower. Once it's used up, we just want to plop down and unwind, which brings us to pleasure's most seductive quality . . .

Third, pleasures require almost zero mental effort to derive happiness from. To enjoy a beer, all we need is a bottle opener (or a talented belly button). To enjoy shopping, all we need is a credit card and an Internet connection. To enjoy Netflix, all we need to do is pick a movie, and even *that* is often too hard on our drained brains at the end of the day.

Meanwhile, nearly *all* forms of building true happiness require mental or physical effort. Exercise requires exertion; practicing a passion requires focus and devotion; even having a conversation with a friend requires concentration, listening, processing, responding, and *ugh* . . . *I'm feeling ego-depleted already. Hand me a beer.*

So let's recap the power of pleasures by examining a seemingly innocuous example (and one of my favorites): the Chipotle burrito. First, it's instantly gratifying. Nobody's going to contest that. Second, it's readily available. Chipotle has over two thousand stores and growing.[5] My friend Kara lives directly behind a Chipotle, and we've even gotten them to throw our burritos over the fence to us.

Lastly, a burrito requires no real mental effort to enjoy. If you're too depleted to even interact with the Chipotle staff, you can just order from the app in seconds. Then, the only thing standing between you and sour cream–slathered goodness is speaking your name at the register (or knocking on the fence).

Perhaps this is why Chipotle sells over 600 *million* burritos per year; they've mastered the art of pleasure indulgence through the trifecta of gratification, availability, and effortless acquisition. Many businesses follow this model, and they're specifically targeting our generation with strong results. Compared to Boomers and Xers, we spend the most in convenience stores, buy more energy drinks, and drink the most craft beer. We're also twice as likely to pay for same-day shipping than anyone else.[6]

Perhaps our penchant for pleasures lends to why we've annoyingly been labeled the "Instant Gratification Generation," but if we look around, pleasure addiction is an ageless human problem.[7] Gambling, alcoholism, smoking, obesity, and sex and drug addiction all have roots in pleasure addiction.

Let's look again at why seemingly innocent pleasures are still threatening to our true happiness when overindulged in. They've opened a Chipotle near my house, so I've begun cooking less at home. With Netflix, it's less enticing to read before bed and instead marathon through one of their well-produced TV shows. In the morning, my Keurig instantly brews delicious coffee, so I'm less driven to go on a jog or meditate for energy. Finally, after work, peeking into my friends' social lives on Facebook lessens the necessity and motivation to have a more fulfilling interaction in person.

In essence, we're constantly engineering and surrounding ourselves with things that are subtly drawing us away from our sources of true happiness. **Even if we're not currently suffering from a pleasure *addiction*, chances are we can temper our intake in a few areas and begin reinvesting more heavily in the things in life that matter, build us as people, and provide true happiness.**

Cutting our pleasures may sound like an unappetizing diet, but from the moment we start, we'll begin saving time and money. As for our battle against ego depletion, true happiness won't grow effortlessly right at the start, but as we become happier, our willpower and energy will rise in tandem. We'll start getting in "happiness shape," and building true happiness will become easier and easier.

Our Pleasure Island Flyover

To bring true happiness . . . to bring peace to all, one must first discipline and control one's own mind.

—Buddha

Now, I face a challenge. Because telling you to stop going to Chipotle would be both ineffectual and hypocritical. There's literally a Chipotle burrito on my desk right now. So instead, we're going to fly over Pleasure Island and take an objective look at our favorite modern-day pleasures, how they impact our happiness, and in some cases, how we can even tweak our use of them to build true happiness instead.

First we'll tackle social media—what the happiest country in the world thinks of it, and how to convert it from a bottomless pleasure pit into a useful social tool. Next, we'll expose the processed-food industry by revealing a simple food-science secret, and learn what revelation caused Coke's COO to dry-heave in the streets of Brazil.

Then, we'll look at the evolution of video games from 1990s pajama-party diversions to the digital cocaine they've become today, reverse engineer the formula behind today's most addictive games, and look at why certain games are conductive of true happiness while others aren't. Afterward, we'll learn the surprising science behind binging TV, and lastly, we'll defy *D.A.R.E.* and uncover the scientific truth behind popular recreational drugs—caffeine included—and which ones catalyze, suspend, and even permanently handicap our happiness.

As mentioned earlier, I was once called "Sexy Zuckerberg" by a Japanese sushi chef. What do the positive psychologists have to say about my billionaire doppelganger's creation?

How Social Is Social Media?

Welcome to the Facebar

Imagine you're wrapping up work, feeling drained, and reeling from a recent breakup. Your friend hasn't texted you back, and you've just remembered your favorite show isn't on until tomorrow. As you drive home, melancholia creeps over you like a cold blanket. Naturally, you seek reprieve.

Instead of going home, you limp to a bar called "Facebook." You know hundreds of your friends will be there waiting to share news of their lives; seems like a great place for a pick-me-up.

You walk in, and intermixed with your friends are casual acquaintances and friends of friends, many of whom you've forgotten about. You begin scanning through the room, seeking respite with good company. You spot your best friend from high school and approach her.

"Hey, Steph, I'm feeling kind of down, what's—"

"MY BOYFRIEND, TOM, AND I HAD A GREAT WEEKEND AT THE LAKE, SEE?" She then waves in your face a Polaroid of her clutching Tom on a Jet Ski, both of them sporting massive grins. "HASHTAG SUNSHINE!"

You offer a forced smile, and move on to your friend from college.

"Hey, Gabe, what're you up—"

"JUST GOT MY MASTERS IN ZOOLOGY, WOOT WOOT!"

A third of the room turns to flash Gabe a thumbs-up. You can no longer ignore the pandemonium around you. As you scan the room, couples stare back at you with wide grins. People stand in their chairs and spout political pontifications to no one in particular. A man flexes in front of you and shouts, "PROGRESS PIC!" You brush past him only to come face-to-face with your beautiful friend in her swimsuit alongside four of her even *more* beautiful friends. After a brief bout of giggles, they shout, "Hashtag beach life! Hashtag Maui!"

Everyone seems so happy, and since nobody's talking to you, you slink out of the room and drive home.

When was the last time going through your Facebook news feed actually made you feel *better* about yourself? In theory, social media sites should be conducive to true happiness; after all, they have *social* in the name, and they instantly connect us with people in our personal networks from around the world. **If used correctly, social media can *lead* to meaningful, in-person social interaction; but is soaking in this torrent of social content providing true happiness itself?**

Why We Love Likes

In his book *Hooked: How to Build Habit-Forming Products,* Stanford professor Nir Eyal reverse engineers social-media sites to help startups create addictive user platforms. Though his formula for addiction potential reads like a success recipe for aspiring app designers, it's more like a warning for us, like the nutrition facts of a Cinnabon.

According to Professor Eyal, Facebook, Twitter, and Instagram keep us hooked with the following four ingredients:

- A trigger (a notification or a reminder to tend to our account)
- An action (a prompt for us to post/comment/like, i.e., Facebook's "What's on your mind?" in the blank status box)
- An unpredictable reward (such as likes, comments, or interesting photos)
- An investment (i.e., a commitment from us, like sharing photos or writing a restaurant review)[8]

The investment, he writes, helps restart the loop—we post a photo, someone likes it, we get a notification, unlock our phones, and suddenly we're back on Facebook. But the *most* addictive element is that unpredictable reward. We all love posting a status and checking back periodically throughout the day to tally our likes and smirk at our friends' clever or supportive comments.

Problem is, these situations activate our amygdala and striatum, brain regions involved in impulsive and addictive behavior. The more we use social media, the more impulsive we become. Likes, followers, and comments aren't much different than a dose of caffeine or other drug; we crave them, feel a relief when we get them, then crave more tomorrow.

Take it from Essena O'Neill, an amateur Australian model who grew a career out of social-media attention. At her peak in 2015, the nineteen-year-old had 800,000 followers on Instagram and 270,000 subscribers on YouTube. She had well-paying sponsors and even multiple offers to join international modeling agencies. Essena had effectively *won* social media, and was making a living off of likes.

"You'd think getting 100,000 followers on Instagram would be amazing," she confesses. "It was, for the day, but then you'd want 200,000. Everything I did was for likes, for followers." To sate her appetite for more positive attention, Essena had begun obsessively and meticulously curating her social media presence. One seemingly spontaneous bikini selfie, she admits, was retaken over one hundred times. She once received a dress in the mail with a bulleted list of instructions on exactly how to pose, smile, and what time of day to upload the picture, along with a check for four hundred dollars.

Then, one day, she deleted everything. Left behind were a handful of her more popular photos with new captions shedding light on her true feelings as a social-media queen. Essena says she martyred her online persona in part to help quit her clawing social-media addiction cold turkey. She also asserts that our news feeds aren't reflective of real life—rather, they're curated highlight reels, lending to feelings of competitiveness and isolation. "We think having likes on Facebook, YouTube, and Instagram creates self-assurance and happiness. It doesn't; it creates dependency," Essena says.[9]

Social media feeds also create unrealistic standards for everything from body image to relationships to travel. When you quickly scroll through your news feed and see a muscular selfie, a beautiful couple holding hands, and a study-abroad student riding a giraffe, you may wonder, *Damn, why am I not jacked, holding hands with someone beautiful—on a giraffe? Where did I go so wrong?!*

Consider Anne and Dave as examples: friends of my friends who dated all throughout college. Their Facebook accounts were constantly updated with adorable shots of them holding hands, huddling together over hot chocolate, and posing in front of national monuments. One photo of them smooching at the foot of the Eiffel Tower as Anne's leg popped in the air solicited a mountain of likes and solidified them as king and queen of the news feed. From Facebook alone, they appeared to be a dream couple. But I knew them better.

In reality, Dave was controlling and Anne was unpredictable. Their Facebook presence was like a luxury home built on North Korea's southern border: a total façade.

One time, Anne and Dave got into an argument outside of his apartment, and a patrolling cop walked up to catch Anne *kneeing Dave in the balls*. Her finishing move got her arrested and charged by the state with assault. Another night, Dave brought a pizza back to Anne's dorm and caught her talking on the phone. I suppose he assumed there was a handsome, thong-wearing Italian man on the other side, because he viciously demanded to know who she was talking to. When she refused to tell him, he angrily launched the pizza out the window and stormed out. Except the window wasn't open, so after performing a midair escape from the box, the pizza slapped onto it and gently slid down as we watched it like a sad Lifetime movie.

Now if Anne felt compelled to inject a dose of reality into her online presence, she might've posted a picture of the situation with the caption "Dave can be a total dick sometimes—*just look at this vertical pizza.*" But no; **Anne and Dave, like an overwhelming majority of us, use social media not as a tool to reflect our humdrum daily lives, but as a way to keep up appearances to a wide audience.**

Our subconscious need to show our best selves is nothing new; psychologists call it "impression management," and social media has simply become an efficient and competitive outlet for subtly one-upping each other.[10]

Impression management has an especially severe effect on those of us in relationships. A University of Mississippi-Columbia study found that high levels of Facebook usage amongst couples often led to jealousy, in turn leading to conflict, cheating, and breakups. "Cutting back to moderate, healthy levels of Facebook usage," says lead researcher Russell Clayton, "could help reduce conflict, particularly for newer couples who are still learning about each other."[11]

Are we really surprised by this, though? Could you imagine if our grandparents did the period equivalent of Facebook-stalking each other and dug up old Polaroids of one another spooning exes at the beach, sharing milkshakes with mysterious suitors, and generally having a grand ol' time without them? To me, that activity sounds more miserable and tense than watching an Adam Sandler movie with a live tiger. And yet, social media makes it *so easy* that it's hard to resist.

But resist we should; Essena, Anne, and Dave show how social media can not only soak up our free time, but consume us with impression management, addiction, and a warped sense of reality. Pretty damning stuff, but let's remember that all three are extreme examples, centering their *lives* around their online presence. Can social media be enjoyed in small, less frequent doses, like a Coke or a burger? And how do we use it to build true happiness?

The Facebook Happiness Quotient

In 2015, the Danish Happiness Research Institute conducted a study where they asked over a thousand "normal" social-media users (who check or post a few things per day) to go on a one-week purge, no checking Facebook allowed. Their objective was to *quantify* how much Facebook affects our happiness.

The results of the purge read like the effects of a miracle drug. Compared to their control group counterparts who continued normal Facebook usage, the group who quit for a week reported:

- Less sadness
- Less loneliness
- Less envy
- Less worry
- Less depression
- Increased enthusiasm
- Increased decisiveness
- Increased focus
- Increased real-life social activity
- Increased satisfaction with their own social lives

At the bottom of the report, the penny drops with a hard clang: by the DHRI's measure, Facebook users are 39 percent less happy than their non-Facebook-using friends. **The report concludes: "after one week without Facebook the treatment group reported** *a significantly higher level of life satisfaction* **[emphasis theirs]."** Then, the Danish scientists dropped their mics, which probably shattered, because I assume everything in Denmark is made of Legos.[12]

To Quit or Not to Quit?

At this point it would be easy for me to urge you to delete your Facebook and go frolic in the nearest meadow. Doing so will probably make you happier overall, but I think abandoning social media entirely would be throwing the baby out with the bathwater. If we look past the jealousy-inducing selfies, creepily tailored banner ads, and relentless Candy Crush invites, Facebook and Twitter can be social Swiss Army knives. We'll get to Instagram soon.

Facebook Chat offers us a way to connect with friends old and new, and has been essential to me in the writing of this book. Facebook also reminds us of our friends' birthdays. (But *don't* write on their wall, because what's that worth? *Call* them.) The site also lets us easily connect with groups and businesses we love. I once reached out to a new band to share my love of their debut EP; my comments and others' inspired the band to stay together and write more material. Plus, Facebook helps you create and track events to facilitate meaningful in-person experiences.

Twitter allows us to track live news faster than most websites can update, and connects us with customer service faster than calls or email. Delta, for example, has over forty employees monitoring the @Delta account to help stranded travelers make connections, while @Healthtap offers advice from real medical professionals.

What about Instagram? Surely a platform plastered with puppies, inspirational quotes, and hot people at the beach is harmless at worst? Nope. Turns out, Instagram has no agreed-upon benefits within the scientific community, making it the cigarette of social media. Reason being, it focuses on the single most happiness-crushing element of other social media platforms. "You get more explicit and implicit cues of people being happy, rich, and successful from a photo than from a status update," says Hanna Krasnova of Humboldt University in Berlin. "A photo can very powerfully provoke immediate social comparison, and that can trigger feelings of inferiority. You don't envy a news story."[12] So be *very* careful who you follow on Instagram; drop the attention-seekers and focus on curating a feed of meaningful content.

That brings us to my practical advice for using social media to build true happiness. At this point, if you've decided to keep your Facebook account, it's probably for one or more of the reasons I decided to keep mine—to track events, check up on close friends, save pictures in the cloud, and pre-screen dates to look for red flags, like Confederate flags or evidence of more than two cats. So, what can we do to cut through the junk and use Facebook, Twitter, or Instagram to amplify, not stymy, our happiness?

First, begin unfollowing people or groups that don't interest you. As you go down your news feed, ask yourself, *Do I really care about this person's life? Do their posts make me happy or jealous? Have their posts ever improved my day?* If they don't make you happy, then unfollow them. Be *unrelenting* in your unfollowing of groups and people who don't make you happy. Over time, this exercise will whittle down your news feed to a stream of meaningful content from the people and groups you care about. I'm friends with over 1,200 people on Facebook, but only *follow* about 150 people closest to me; that way, my news feed is a highlight reel of updates from only the people and groups I care most about.

If you find that *nothing* on your news feed interests you, just stay away from it entirely. After all, the news feed is *endless*; it has no natural stopping point, so it takes discipline or distractions to pull us away. Most of the time, it's better never to enter the news feed at all.

Next, try logging into social media only when you have an explicit purpose in mind, like messaging someone in particular, reviewing some pictures of a friend's wedding, or posting a status. We oftentimes log onto social media for the hell of it because we're in a state of boredom, stress, or are avoiding responsibilities. Indulging on social-media content is a potent form of procrastination we should avoid; there are much better ways to spend those five minutes we have free (for ideas, see my short eBook *ASAP Happiness: 25 Ways to Build Happiness in 5 Minutes*).

Lastly, disable your desktop and phone notifications. Remember, the first element of Professor Eyal's "hooked" methodology is the trigger, and we should take advantage of our ability to disable it.

Essena is now writing a book satirizing social-media fame called *How to Be Social Media Famous*. Though she can barely afford rent, she posted a video of herself beaming with joy and excitement at her newfound life purpose. "Social media is not real life," she says. "Meeting people . . . talking to people, hugging people, going to the park and enjoying nature . . . that's real life." If we can temper our usage and stay away from black holes of low-value content, we can repurpose social media for our benefits: as a conductor for meaningful connections and true happiness.

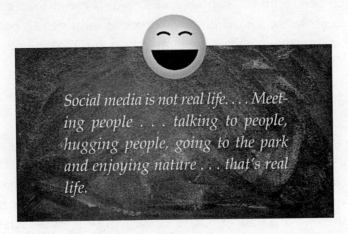

Social media is not real life. . . . Meeting people . . . talking to people, hugging people, going to the park and enjoying nature . . . that's real life.

Food: A Recipe for True Happiness

Even the frying of bacon sounds like applause.

—Jim Gaffigan

Ah, food—a simple pleasure we can't live without. We may very well be the most food-obsessed culture in the world, able to order and sample international cuisine without getting out of our pajamas. A tremendously competitive culinary industry constantly produces tastier and more unique offerings for our palates across all price ranges, from five-star restaurants to the frozen-food aisle. Our taste buds have sampled more variety than that of Alexander the Great. In America, we have an entire *television network* devoted to food *on basic cable*.

This section isn't going to be rife with what Jim Gaffigan calls "kale propaganda." Nor will it be a sacred-cow barbeque of everything we love to eat (though sacred-cow burgers sound *delicious*). Instead, in this section we'll blow open the processed-food industry and learn why synthetic snacks are so bad for our happiness. Then, we'll cover the true happiness of food, wrapping up with a simple eating trick from the happiest, healthiest people in the world.

So let's talk processed food. I have my favorites and so do you; mine happen to be Dr. Pepper and Reese's Peanut Butter Cups. These treats make for delightful occasional indulgences between nutritious meals. Problem is, some companies that make them aren't satisfied with just being "occasional" anymore.

Bet You Can't Eat Just One!

The Lay's potato chips slogan, which has been in use since 1963, is more accurate than you might think. Food scientists describe potato chips, among other crave-inducing treats, as "hyperpalatable," blending an unholy trinity of fat, salt, and sugar. Our brains naturally release a flow of pleasure-inducing chemicals when we eat, and these foods maximize that flow.

In 2011, American food scientists found that hyperpalatable foods trigger many of the same pathways in the brain as addictive drugs, such as compulsion, addiction, and withdrawal.[13] In fact, a 2007 study by French food scientists found that 94 percent of lab rats preferred water tinged with a common artificial sweetener to water sprinkled with *cocaine*. Shocked by the results, the scientists pumped even *more* cocaine into the latter sample, yet the rats *still* preferred the sugar water. Meanwhile, the cocaine rats are still in rehab alongside several rock stars.[14]

So rats love our junk food, but contrary to popular belief, *humans* in America have always harbored disdain for our processed-food industry, and on several occasions have even acted out in open rebellion.

America saw burgeoning anti-junk food movements in the 1980s, with particular venom aimed at Oscar Mayer. The inventors of the Weinermobile faced tough times after health-food advocates chose bologna as a prime target, citing ridiculously high sodium and cholesterol levels. But **rather than engineer a healthier sandwich** stuffer, Oscar Mayer simply repackaged bologna with crackers and cheese and sold it to the same busy moms as premade lunches for their kids. Thus, the Lunchable was born. The anti-bologna movement continued, but the ruse had worked; Lunchables exploded into a varied product line in the 1990s, boasting over $1 billion in sales. Today, Lunchables are so unhealthy that even the inventor's grandchildren aren't allowed to eat them.

Needless to say, big food companies generally haven't had our best interests in mind. Pulitzer Prize–winning journalist Michael Moss uncovered that Lunchables family secret while investigating for his book *Salt Sugar Fat: How the Food Giants Hooked Us.* In it, he also interviews Jeffrey Dunn, Coke's former president and COO of the Americas from the early 2000s. During Dunn's tenure, Coke was designing a twenty-cent, 6.7-oz. bottle specifically targeted at the poorest regions of South America. When Dunn visited his target audience in the favelas of Rio, he reported dry-heaving from guilt. "These people need a lot of things, but they don't need a Coke."

Upon his return to Coke HQ in Atlanta, he championed an effort to steer Coke's marketing efforts in a more responsible direction by first pulling advertising for Coke out of public schools, which were (and still are) suffering an obesity epidemic. Stakeholders in Coke, namely bottlers, labeled Dunn a heretic, and the board had him fired immediately. "They're a very, very aggressive company," he says. While Coke's mission statement reads, "Refresh the world in mind, body, and spirit," Dunn insists they're really more interested in outselling Pepsi, then milk, then *water*.[15]

Narcotic Nourishment

How on earth could Coke outsell *water*? Never mind that they gave up and created Dasani in 1999. Point is, isn't our body smart enough to ask for more *water* than *soda*? It was, for a while. Then Coke and other processed-food companies got smarter.

In the 1970s the military was developing a more sophisticated ration to issue soldiers in the field called the Meal Ready to Eat, or

MRE. But almost immediately, the developers found themselves in a pickle. Soldiers were getting bored with eating the same twelve entrées over and over, and were discarding half-eaten rations, missing out on essential calories.

Research into the problem revealed that the soldiers preferred the flavorful entrées over the bland bread products at *first*, but once "MRE fatigue" set in, they only ate the most mundane, flavorless items in the ration and tossed the chicken tetrazzini out of the Humvee window.

Why would the soldiers get tired of eating the most enriching items so quickly? Why is it that we don't mind eating some form of bread with every meal, but the thought of eating Five Guys thrice in a row nauseates us? With further research into the vexing question, Harvard food scientist Howard Moskowitz uncovered a game-changer for the processed-food industry: *sensory-specific satiety*.[16]

Basically, our brains are wired to detect when we've had too much of a certain flavor and suppress our desire for more. As we evolved, this helped guide a balanced diet from multiple food sources, meaning at some point as our ancestor gnawed on a delicious speared goat, his brain went, "Enough, Oonga. Go find a carrot."

Following Moskowitz's discovery, major food companies began engineering their products around what industry insiders call "the bliss point": the perfect offering of taste and addictiveness without any specific revealing flavor. **They realize that our brains can't tell us to stop eating something if they can't figure out what "it" is.**

Food companies go to great lengths to achieve the bliss point for each product. For example, the Dr. Pepper Snapple Group organized four thousand tasting events of Dr. Pepper Cherry Vanilla before finalizing the flavor.

But food companies weren't satisfied with addictive taste alone. Frito-Lay developed a $40,000 chewing-simulation machine to optimize the crispiness of their chip formulas for peak oral stimulation (turns out it's four pounds per square inch). The puffy Cheeto, according to food scientist Dr. Steven Witherly, "is one of the most marvelously constructed foods on the planet, in terms of pure pleasure." According to Dr. Witherly, the Cheeto melts in our mouth to trick the body into thinking we're consuming fewer calories than we really are. This is a phenomenon called "vanishing caloric density," or VSD. Other snacks exploiting VSD are french fries, ice cream, and popcorn; things that make us say, "Okay, someone take these away from me."

Vanishing caloric density and sensory-specific satiety are only two of dozens of food-perception theories Dr. Witherly outlines in his study *Why Humans Like Junk Food*.[17] The report lays out the whole arsenal of tricks the processed-food industry uses to dazzle our palates and keep us coming back for more.

Again, I'm not propagating kale and this book wasn't partially paid for by Pickle Packers International (a real group). Processed food is delicious, convenient, cheap, and won't kill us or our happiness in small doses. I myself enjoy a zesty Pepsi and indulge in a Snickers here and there. **But before we tip that sleeve of Oreos into our mouths while making wood-chipper noises, we should never forget that many of our favorite treats are *engineered* to bypass our bodies' natural defenses against overeating.**

Take it from Daniel, who at age eighteen weighed 360 pounds. Throughout high school he had always dreamed of losing weight, but processed foods had a firm grip on him. "Apathy is by far the most dangerous emotion, especially when it comes to food," he told me. "I wouldn't even realize that I just ate through an entire family-sized bag of chips on my own. That's how dangerous apathy is."

Daniel's story has a happy ending we'll cover in the next chapter, but for now, the takeaway is this: next time we treat ourselves to some Wendy's or Doritos, let's remember that our brains have a really hard time asking us to stop eating artificial food. It's up to our own volition and continued dedication to long-term happiness to exercise restraint and balance our intake with exercise and organic, freshly prepared foods.

Generation Yum

Thankfully, many of us already know how to convert food into happiness. Compared to our parents' generation, our food choices tend to be healthier, more natural, less processed, but also more expensive. That last bit doesn't stop us, however; half of us identify as "foodies" and eat out, on average, more than once a week, often in a social setting. "Never has a young generation paid *this* much attention to food," says author Eve Turow Paul.

In her book *A Taste of Generation Yum*, she reveals how we're the first young generation to spend more on food than clothes. We've also supported a 174 percent rise in farmers' markets from 2000 to 2012 and author most of the forty thousand new food blogs started in the last five years.[18] Go us!

Never has a young generation paid this much attention to food.

This brings us to a crossroads in our happiness training. Yes, the *consumption* of food is unequivocally a pleasure. When our bodies process food, our brains release chemicals that stimulate our pleasure sensors. Plenty of food today is engineered to maximize pleasure while circumventing our body's natural moderation systems, making food an often challenging pleasure to enjoy in healthy moderation.

However, I can't think of a pleasure more conducive to true happiness than food, not even social media. Every day it catalyzes social behavior as we enjoy meals in each other's company. It serves as a powerful bridge between cultures as we travel. It inspires us to learn the culinary arts, and for those of us with the creative bug it serves as a muse for cooking and writing. For many of us, a love of food has even brought and kept loved ones close.

So on a daily basis, what can we do to maximize the true happiness *and* pleasure food provides?

Hara Hachi Bun Me

The answer lies in one of the world's Blue Zones: tiny, peculiar regions where inhabitants enjoy measurably longer lifespans.

There are currently five Blue Zones in the world: the Italian island of Sardinia, a peninsula jutting out from Costa Rica called Nicoya, a Greek island called Icaria, a tiny town in California called Linda Loma, and the subject of our study, the Japanese island of Okinawa. In addition to longer lifespans, Okinawans report tremendous levels of life satisfaction, brought about by social and altruistic behavior, exercise, and healthy eating. Do they wash down a fanatical vegan diet with water from the Fountain of Youth? Nope; Okinawans are total omnivores, eating plenty of meat and sweets. One famous island saying says it all: "Every part of a pig can be eaten except its hooves and its 'oink.'"

Okinawans' secret is their simple eating code called "hara hachi bun me," loosely translated to "eat until you are eight parts (of ten) full." Their philosophy echoes an old Japanese proverb: *Eight parts of a full stomach sustain the man; the other two sustain the doctor.*[19] In addition to their eating code, Okinawans have the highest proportion of living centenarians (people 100+ years old), have 80 percent less chance of heart disease than Westerners, and many boast the percentage body fat of Derek Zoolander.

Coincidence? Scientists say no; *hara hachi bun me* plays a critical role. Okinawans simply eat how we're all *supposed* to eat.

In their book *The Mindful Diet*, researchers from the Duke Integrative Medicine Center describe how our stomachs are only designed to be about 80 percent full of food. Our bodies are programmed with a trigger to tell us when we've reached that point, like how a gas pump shuts off once the tank is sufficiently full. But while the latter is conveniently instantaneous, our stomach's shutoff valve is on a delay of about fifteen minutes.[20]

We eat quickly in Western culture, and oftentimes by the time our body signals us to stop, we've already eaten too much. As a result, our stomach has no room for water and gases to begin the digestion process, so it expands to make more room. To us, the extra space often feels like a "second wind," or an opportunity to polish off that burger or take a last swig of Coke Zero. After all, it's no good to waste food, right? But if our stomachs could spew profanity at this point, they would.

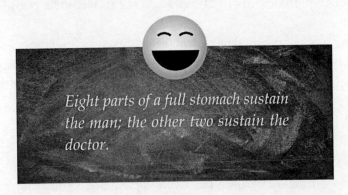

Eight parts of a full stomach sustain the man; the other two sustain the doctor.

When we fill this emergency space with *more* food, we force our stomachs to expand *again*, leading to severe discomfort and bloating. This effect is called postprandial somnolence, or PPS, commonly known as a food coma. During PPS, our parasympathetic nervous system goes into emergency mode, redirecting blood away from the rest of the body to assist with digesting the oversized load of food. The loss of blood flow around the body results in the feeling of weakness and light-headedness, forcing us to crawl out of Five Guys.

For the Love of Food

So how can we maximize true happiness from food, and avoid pleasure-based pitfalls like food comas? First and foremost, follow the Okinawan code of *hara hachi bun me*, and slow down your eating so your body has time to signal when you're happily 80 percent full. This will take practice, but the payoff is tremendous—you'll save food, money, and feel more energetic throughout the day. We'll go deeper into the practice of "mindful eating" in Chapter 6.

Also, be careful around processed foods. Remember that the simple Dorito is the culmination of decades of research and engineering with our addiction and wallet—not our health—in mind. Lastly, let's *use* our love of food to help us build true happiness.

Take a cooking class, try a new restaurant with a friend, etc. Or as my fellow agent of happiness Charlie Hoehn, author of *Recession Proof Graduate* puts it, "Love each meal, with the people you love."

Food has been our friend since the dawn of existence, and is poised now more than ever to help us build a healthy, happy life. Through smart food choices and *hara hachi bun me*, let's nourish not only our pleasure sensors but our bodies, minds, and happiness as well.

Video Games: Our Constantly On/Off Relationship

Video games are perhaps our newest pleasure. While they started out decades ago as primitive digital diversions, they've since evolved into a prominent entertainment medium; a canvas for complex storytelling, unprecedented immersion, and even artistic expression. Interactive digital worlds have allowed us to live out wild, rewarding fantasies, and for some of us, those fantasies have become preferable to real life. Do video games have a place in our happiness-building toolkit? Or should we take a hard pass on PlayStation?

A Nerd's Journey Begins

In 1996 I received my first video game, *Donkey Kong Land*, with a brand-new, crimson-red Game Boy Pocket. I took my prized Game Boy to the lake with some family friends and never took my eyes off of it, walking into walls, lamps, and almost the lake itself. I, like many other elementary schoolers, was instantly hooked.

I was fairly confident I'd get *Pokémon Red* for my birthday in September because I made a habit of begging for it at least four hours every day. In giddy anticipation of my birthday, I asked my best friend, Joseph, to lend me his paper Pokédex (Pokémon glossary), and with it I planned out my entire adventure: which Pokémon I'd start out with, how I'd approach each gym leader, and how I'd beat each of my friends' favorite Pokémon.

Ironically, an unwavering fervor for the Pokémon video game served as a prerequisite to a social life back then, as it bonded third-graders together through a common language. I distinctly remember my friend Paul breaking an EXIT sign at summer camp and offering me a rare Blastoise card to take the blame. I did, but sadly, the water Pokémon didn't survive a dip in the pool that afternoon.

In the late 1990s our ideal Friday night had us surrounding a friend's TV and Nintendo 64, slipping into digital bliss before games like *Mario Kart, Star Fox,* and *Super Smash Brothers.* Four of us could play on one TV together, and those who weren't playing would cheer, jeer, and shout what little profanity we knew in excitement. Games back then were brilliant, but they didn't hold our attention forever. Instead, they fit nicely into a natural rotation of activities, alongside pillow fort–making, reading *Calvin & Hobbes,* and finding a way to get covered in mud before Mom picked us up. **After all, games back in the 1990s were limited by their simplicity; Nintendo 64 games could only be up to sixty-four megabytes in size, or barely enough to hold a modern smartphone's emoji library.**

However, gaming changed in the early 2000s. With a wave of more-powerful home consoles and bigger development budgets, games became more interesting, more complex, and demanded more of our time before the credits rolled. The new hardware combined with faster Internet also allowed us to play each other online and challenge gamers from around the world. Suddenly we no longer had to convene at a friend's house to enjoy games together, and due to the novelty of fighting new human foes in every match, we had little reason to stop playing. I'd play *Halo 2* for hours, honing my avatar's lethality whether my friends were online or not. By high school, my friends and I had become thoroughbred gamers. And we weren't alone, because by the mid-2000s, skyrocketing sales of video games solidified them as a juggernaut entertainment medium.

Since then, video games have become the dominant pillar of the entertainment industry, toppling a record held by Hollywood since the 1920s. Over 155 million Americans play video games, and Millennials like us make up over a third of that statistic, meaning *most* of us play games. Furthermore, we've solidified games as our preferred mode of entertainment over music, movies, and television. We spend most of our entertainment budget on games, and 57 percent of us report gaming three-plus hours per week.[21]

We love games so much we even enjoy watching complete strangers play them online. **The gameplay-streaming platform Twitch accounts for 43.6 percent of all live-streamed Internet content, compared to ESPN's 6.3 percent and CNN's 0.8 percent.[22] That means we'd rather watch PewDiePie get mauled in *Dark Souls III* than watch NFL highlights or even *the news*.**

We love to shoot Nazi zombies as much as the Greatest Generation loved to shoot *actual Nazis*. So the question is this: is all of this gaming really good for us?

Brain Broccoli

Cognitive neuroscientist Dr. Daphne Bavelier studies what she calls the "broccoli" side of video games—the underlying health benefits—in order to guide development for games oriented toward education and rehabilitation. She found that action games like *Call of Duty* and *Halo* increase our ability to distinguish small details, double our objects of attention (i.e., number of objects in motion our brains can track at once), improve our multitasking skills, and reduce our reaction times.[23]

Other games allow us to exercise our creativity. Will Wright, the designer of *The Sims*, sees games as "an amplifier of the player's imagination."[24] His Darwinian adventure game *Spore* allows players to design and evolve an organism from a single cell to an intergalactic civilization. Since the game's release in 2008, players have created and shared nearly 200 million unique creatures (and a whopping *third* of them aren't at all phallic).

For some of us, video games have had a profound impact on the direction of our lives. Carlos, twenty-four, grew up captivated by the interactivity of video games. Unlike in books or movies, video games allowed him to change the outcome of the story. He studied game design in school and is now the narrative director of an independent gaming studio. Elly, thirty-one, met her husband discussing video games at a bar. Her love for games has also inspired her to learn to sew so she could create video game–themed costumes for conventions and parties.

Unlike television or movies, games more directly connect us with people from around the globe. The online multiplayer menu in *Halo* displays a world map with lights to indicate where online players are located (there are always two lights in Moscow, which I assume is Putin and his well-trained bear). Some connections are meaningful; games like *Rainbow Six* and *Starcraft* necessitate team-work and communication in order to succeed. A handful of gamers have even found their significant others while playing popular online roleplaying games like *World of Warcraft* or *Second Life*.

So video games seem to inspire us, connect us, and captivate us, perhaps even more than other entertainment mediums. Does that mean they'd make a healthy addition to our campaign for true happiness? Not always, because to offer these infrequent, often fringe benefits, video games demand a high price in return.

Neural Chocolate

Dr. Bavelier describes the unhealthy side of video games as the "chocolate" side—where publishers and designers maximize the elements of addictiveness and irresistibility that has exploded videogames into a nearly $100 billion industry.

Tom Chatfield, gaming theorist and author of *Fun, Inc.*, has been reverse engineering massively popular games like *World of Warcraft* and *Call of Duty* for over a decade to understand how they sell so well year after year. He's learned that the designers of these games have meticulously implemented worlds "which tick our evolutionary boxes."[25] Similar to how processed food is engineered to light up our palate, games light up our brains. To keep us hooked, modern game designers mix a seductive digital cocktail with some, or oftentimes *all*, of the following ingredients:

1) An experience bar to measure our progress
2) Multiple simultaneous short- and long-term objectives
3) A reward for effort, even if we lose
4) Feedback, usually in the form of a ranking system
5) An element of uncertainty, luck, and chance, like randomized rewards

Interestingly, the defining games of our childhood like *Mario Kart 64* and *Super Smash Bros.* included one or *none* of these things, yet we still loved them all the same. That's because these tools don't necessarily make games *better*, they just make them more *addictive*. But who stands to profit from a more addictive game? Cue the hippie running around your room screaming, "It's the corporations, man!"

Just how *much* have video games profited from this addictive formula? Blizzard Entertainment, creators of the online fantasy game *World of Warcraft*, continue to rake in $800 million a year from subscription fees alone for a game they made in 2004. The military action series *Call of Duty*, which now releases a new title annually, has generated nearly $12 billion in sales—*triple* what Disney paid for the rights to *Star Wars*. Mobile games especially are benefitting from this formula. *Candy Crush* generated $1.8 billion in sales in 2013. *Clash of Clans* creator Supercell has been valued at $3 billion. Interestingly, both mobile games are free to get, and have generated revenue strictly from gamers continuing to buy optional game content. Never-ending video games, it seems, are the most lucrative carrot-on-a-stick scheme of all time.

All of the gamers I interviewed admitted to chasing the carrot for too long at least once in their lives. Matt, twenty-five, is a successful entrepreneur in Atlanta. Early in his freshman year of college, he picked up a copy of *Call of Duty: Modern Warfare 2* and began playing to his heart's content, free from his parents' wagging fingers. Within seven months, he had played thirty-four days online—

roughly a quarter of his waking hours. "Once I realized, I stopped and thought 'I'm going to regret wasting all of this time,'" he says.

Karsten, thirty-three, played the online roleplaying game *Everquest* for up to six hours a day while he attended high school in Germany. "My life did not fall apart," he affirms, "but I missed out on a lot of opportunities that passed me by while a significant chunk of my life was sacrificed to made-up progress in a virtual world."

Matt and Karsten's epiphanies testify to scientists' views on gaming. Dr. Stuart Brown, author of *Play*, feels video games hold back our social development. **"The intense visual stimuli that screens provide, along with a captivating narrative, can be very seductive playmates . . . [but] when someone is gaming and watching a screen, there is no engagement in the natural world, no development of the social nuances that are part of maturation in us as a social species."**[26] So the problem isn't so much what we're *doing* when we game, it's what we're *not* doing—being social and developing ourselves.

Following their release from gaming's grip, both men continued on to successful, happier lives. Today, Karsten helps tech entrepreneurs scale their businesses and has been featured in *Inc.* magazine.[III] Matt picked up amateur boxing and runs a successful nonprofit benefitting dozens of other charities. Both men assert Dr. Brown's theory that video games were holding them back. "I saw them as an outlet for a surplus of ambition rather than a leak through which ambition drained," admits Karsten. Matt used them as an escape from the daunting social demands of college. "If they become a crutch, a getaway, a way for you to shirk passions or responsibilities, that's when video games are bad."

Our reliance on video games as an escape goes back as far as games in general have been around. Around 2,500 years ago, a kingdom called Lydia in modern-day Turkey was suffering from a famine. The king, desperate for a solution, created the first dice

---

[III] You can read his blog and full story of how he kicked his gaming addiction on his website: https://www.karstenaichholz.com/life/video-game-addiction/.

from sheep knuckles. By kingdom-wide decree, everyone would eat on one day and play dice the next, then eat, then play. In theory, they'd be so immersed in the blissful escapism the games provided, they'd forget their hunger during the gaming days. The plan worked, and the kingdom survived an eighteen-year famine this way.[27]

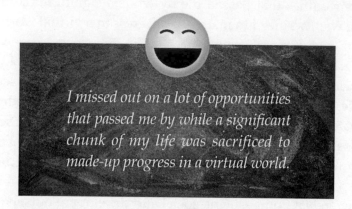

I missed out on a lot of opportunities that passed me by while a significant chunk of my life was sacrificed to made-up progress in a virtual world.

In today's Western society, we don't face the needs of a universally starving populace (nor do we get punched by sheep anymore. Thanks, Lydia.), and as we leave our parents' nests and become more in control of our own lives, our happiness and success stems from our personal growth, pursuit of new experiences, and exploration of passions. Video games are *powerful* distractions from those goals. By tapping into our evolutionary needs, modern games keep us hooked longer, rewarding us with fleeting feelings of accomplishment and satisfaction in exchange for gluts of our valuable time. While they certainly provide some benefits, they can't compete with a life built around experiences, interaction, and growth.

That's absolutely not to say games should be entirely eradicated from our entertainment diet. Dr. Bavelier compares games to wine; if consumed in small doses, they can relax us and even provide a pinch of benefits. But imbibe too much, and the negatives start to outweigh the positives.

I also happen to think some games like *Super Smash Bros.*, *Bioshock*, and *Resident Evil 4* have aged like a fine wine.

Gaming for Good

Before we move on, are there any games out there that may be considered more conductive of true happiness? What games, if any, do happy and successful people play?

Matt plays online chess to sharpen his strategic thinking, and plays short sessions of *Minecraft*, a popular world-building game, to flex his creativity. Elon Musk, CEO of Tesla Motors and SpaceX, enjoys *Kerbal Space Program*, a game about designing and launching rockets he calls "awesome."[28]

Mark Cuban, billionaire owner of the Dallas Mavericks and *Shark Tank* investor, is a self-proclaimed "noob" at the online strategy game *League of Legends*, but enjoys it, calling it "five-dimensional chess against the world." He once attended a *League of Legends* charity match where he dropped the f-bomb on camera and was promptly fined $15,000. When asked if he'd like to up it to $30,000, he said, "F*** it."[29]

As for yours truly, I'm a former video game addict myself. I dumped a regrettable number of hours into *Call of Duty* and *World of Warcraft* in high school and freshman year of college, hours I don't care to add up in my mind. But like Matt, Karsten, and most of my old gaming buddies, I realized the time and effort I was investing could be better spent furthering my ambitions and goals. I still play casually, but nowhere near the levels I used to, because had I continued harvesting so much fleeting pleasure from video games, this book wouldn't exist.

Television: Are We HBOverdosing?

> *On Friday night, I was reading my new book, but my brain got tired, so I decided to watch some television instead.*
> —Stephen Chbosky, author of
> *The Perks of Being a Wallflower*

While my fifteen-year love affair with video games may have faded, my love for TV has only strengthened with age like a piece of oak. I'm currently burning through *Last Week Tonight with John Oliver*, and have some *Orange is the New Black* to catch up on next. Suffering a creative drought yesterday, I poured a glass of scotch and watched three and a half hours of *Archer* on Netflix, laughing myself silly at everyone's favorite sociopathic cartoon superspy.

Three and a half hours may *sound* like a lot of TV, but that's exactly our generation's daily watching average. Surely our binging habits taper off as we age and our responsibilities mount, right? Nope; older Millennials with kids watch nearly *five* hours per day.[30] So our love for the boob tube shows no signs of slowing down.

Television has comfortably settled into the daily American diet alongside over-caffeinated coffee, and its overconsumption has likewise been destigmatized. It's the only thing we can routinely ingest heavy doses of without an impending intervention, and oftentimes the worse crime is *not* to be caught up on the latest shows. (*Do you watch* Game of Thrones? *You DON'T? Good luck finding new friends, you philistine!*)

So as TV skyrockets in popularity, questions loom: where did our love for TV spring from? From a scientific perspective, *why* do we love TV so much? And most importantly, how are the hours we spend before the boob tube affecting our true happiness?

Ironically, our burning love for this particular pleasure may have begun in the most unlikely of places: a classroom.

The Birth of Binging

Perhaps the most tingle-inducing, delightful sight for us elementary schoolers in the 1990s was watching our teacher roll the TV stand into the classroom and shuffle through VHS tapes. Once the dusty, rear-projection monitor fizzled to life, anything could come on: *Bill Nye the Science Guy*, *Schoolhouse Rock*, *The Magic School Bus*, or if we were really lucky, the beginning of a *whole movie*. As the lights faded and the TV beamed against the chalkboard background, we joined our classmates in slipping into a semivegetative state, learning be damned.

As we became of Rated-R age, the range of programming on TV drastically widened, as did its accessibility. The relaxed, entranced state we felt as kids now lay mere clicks away on Netflix, Hulu, or Tivo. We could suddenly pay our way around commercials, record content in bulk, or even stream from a nearly endless online library of content. Plus, as the recession shattered the American Dream, TV only got stronger. Just as we did during the Great Depression, America once again turned to cheap pleasures to resuscitate our happiness like a shot of adrenaline. Sales of cigarettes, junk food, movie tickets, and premium-television subscriptions skyrocketed after '08, and as we poured money into our entertainment industry, TV networks could produce more and better shows. Now, statistically, *most* of us have a Netflix subscription,[31] and let's be honest, those of us who don't are probably just using their ex's or parents' account. You know who you are.

So clearly on the pleasure scale, we rate TV extremely highly, right up there with sex and bacon burgers. But why is that? Sex and food sate physiological needs, so their appeal is obvious. So what need could TV *possibly* provide that we spend so many of our waking hours on it?

Narrative Transport

Mythbusters happens to be one of my favorite shows, so let's tackle a long-running myth about TV together:

Myth: Watching TV relieves stress.

Many of you are probably thinking, *Of course it does! Why else would I want to plop down on the couch for some* Walking Dead *after a hard day's work?* Seems logical, too; we watch TV in a relaxed physical position, and unlike video games, TV doesn't require constant input. Shouldn't that be relaxing?

A group of researchers surveying 471 busy Americans found that streaming media after work actually caused "depletion." Respondents found TV-watching to enable procrastination; they described "giving in" to TV, and that this "guilty pleasure" feeling prevented them from benefitting from the downtime and relaxing. The researchers concluded that "ego depletion may increase the risk of negatively appraising the use of entertaining media as a form of procrastination," and that TV "often seems to be a burden and a stressor rather than a recovery resource."[32]

So it seems like watching TV doesn't so much relieve our stress as it *suspends* it, and once the TV's off reality sets back in and we feel like guilty bums. What if we wipe out our to-do list beforehand, *then* flip on the boob tube? If we're *already* relaxed, will TV amplify, or at least prolong, our relaxed state?

The answer is not really . . . to either. In her book *Stressaholic*, Dr. Heidi Hanna walks us through three reasons why TV doesn't relieve stress. First, it takes away from neurologically nourishing activities like cooking, reading, meditating, journaling, and spending time with loved ones. Second, TV close to bedtime causes wakefulness, disrupting our sleeping habits.[33]

Lastly, TV is often *intended* to increase our stress. The news, crime shows, heartbreaking dramas, and violent movies all trigger our body's stress response, increasing our cortisol levels "even if we're not aware of it." This, according to psychologist Michael Tomasello, is because our brains' mirror neurons are "remarkably capable" of putting ourselves in the shoes of others. "The imitative capacities of our minds," writes developmental psychologist Paul Harris, "enable us to almost completely occupy a fictional position." Scientists call our embodiment of characters onscreen "narrative transport."[34]

Here's where binging comes in. A 2014 study found that "binge-watching increased transportation into a narrative," meaning the more we watch in a single sitting, the more we feel sucked into the television, "increasing enjoyment."[35]

So when we watch TV, we're not relieving stress; we're entertaining ourselves by subconsciously living the experiences of the characters onscreen without the associated risk or effort. This is how TV can elicit such genuine human responses, from hysterically laughing at *Rick and Morty*, to fighting tears through *The Fault in Our Stars*, to feeling danger during *Mad Max*.

If TV elicits genuine human emotion, can it generate true happiness? Researchers say yes! Consumers of intellectually stimulating content such as factual shows or documentaries report improved emotional states.[36] It's hard to feel guilty if we've learned something in the process, especially if that new knowledge has inspired us to take action. For example, the documentary *Waiting for Superman* inspired my friend Shawn to pursue a career in education policy changes, while *Cowspiracy* galvanized my friend Grace into treating food and the environment with more care. The documentary *Happy* on Netflix helped inspire me to write this book, and *The Blair Witch Project* inspired my friend Sebastian "never to camp in Maryland."

Roll Credits

The key takeaway here is that TV is a *pleasure, not* a stress reliever. TV will provide short-term happiness, but will only suspend or amplify our stress levels unless we balance our binging with true stress-reducing activities like meditation and exercise. Meditating or jogging before a twilight tube session makes TV better anyhow, since our lowered stress levels and increased focus will boost the effects of narrative transport.

Now, I'm off for a jog before wrapping up season four of *Archer*.

Drugs: The Good, the Bad, and the Happiness Killers

Growing up, watchful parents and the infamous fallacy-propagating D.A.R.E. program deterred us from drugs for months if not whole years before curiosity or peer pressure overcame us. The percentage of Americans that have tried recreational drugs has recently crept past fifty, while weed's enemies are losing ground to science and progressive legislature.[37] Even the import of more hardcore drugs shows no signs of slowing down. It seems we'll always have access to drugs, legal or not, and so will our children, so it's more critical than ever for us to understand how exactly drugs are affecting our minds, bodies, and both short- and long-term happiness.

To begin, let's start out with our *favorite* drug of all: caffeine.

Caffeine: The Fuel of Capitalism

I'm proud to say caffeine is the only drug I've abused to the point of causing my mother to break down in tears. Plus, it was entirely her fault.

When I was five, Mama Butsch offered me a bottle of Mountain Dew on a road trip, mistaking it for Pepsi's equivalent of a caffeine-free Sprite. Having consumed enough caffeine to resurrect a dead horse, I began fidgeting and giggling in the backseat of our family Volvo like a cartoon mental patient. The seat belt proved a solid pediatric straitjacket until my exhausted father opened the door at our destination, prompting me to spring out like a little blonde jackrabbit. For the next several hours my poor mother chased me in and around my grandparents' house, eventually trapping me in a bedroom where I happily bounced off the walls into the wee hours of the night while she wept, reeling from a grievous mistake.

Nowadays, my relationship with caffeine is much healthier. Caffeine is the world's most consumed drug, with around four out of five Americans consuming it daily. This delightful stimulant is legal and unregulated around the world because it's totally safe. After all, to reach lethal levels, or ten grams a day, we'd have to consume over thirty ventis from Starbucks in a single sitting.[38]

So what happens to our brains when we stay well within the limits, and furthermore, what exactly happens when we crash?

The Science of Mind Viagra

Caffeine is a stimulant that blocks the action of the neurotransmitter adenosine, the brain's "party pooper" chemical that stimulates drowsiness and suppresses arousal. After kicking out adenosine, caffeine starts the party by increasing the flow of the neurotransmitters noradrenaline and dopamine, increasing our focus, athletic ability, and yes, happiness!

But the effect, as we all know, is temporary. **The good news is that a caffeine "crash" is nothing sinister; it's just adenosine showing back up to break up the party and returning dopamine**

and adrenaline to their normal levels. You can lessen the effects of a crash by staying hydrated.

So when is caffeine not a fun-loving party starter? Well, like many of our human friends, caffeine doesn't mix well with alcohol. The presence of both substances in your mind creates what toxicologists call "toxic jock" syndrome. Aside from sounding like Spider-Man's next villain, toxic jock is a dangerous state when we feel energized to drink past our limit and partake in dangerous physical activities with fewer inhibitions. Toxic jock has led to drunk driving, sexual assault, and dangerous stunts ending in self-harm and disability. In 2010, the FDA issued warning letters to manufacturers of the four most popular alcoholic energy drinks, including Four Loko, citing caffeine as an "unsafe food additive" to alcoholic beverages. Fearing the wrath of the FDA, all four companies responded by removing all stimulants from their drinks.[39]

Thankfully those beverages were never too popular because we overwhelmingly prefer to get our caffeine fix from coffee. Forty-three percent of American Millennials call coffee our favorite drink, but our java fandom pales in comparison to roughly seventy percent of Millennials in Turkey and South Africa.[40] Here's the icing on the coffee cake: a study by the American Academy of Neurology found that while diet-sweetened beverages increase our risk for depression, coffee *lowers* it.[41]

Ironically, I wasn't a fan of coffee until *after* I left my stressful job. I never drank it growing up and the coffee at work tasted like butt, so to handle the long hours, I drank an energy shot every day, sometimes followed by an energy drink. I knew my intake wasn't sustainable, but the hours never let up so I never found a convenient time to stop. Finally, one day I called my grandfather, a renowned cardiologist, to confess my stim addiction and ask whether I might be doing long-term harm to myself. **"Stop drinking those energy drinks, Christopher, they're full of sugar and crap." Fair enough.** What about the energy shots? "Those are mostly B-vitamins. Whatever you don't use, you'll just piss out."

In his salty wisdom, Grandpa Butsch was right. Energy drinks are the greater enemy of the two, since they're packed with sugar, empty calories, and other additives like ginseng, guarana, and taurine. According to the Mayo Clinic, these extra ingredients *are* linked to increased physical and mental performance, but your average energy drink doesn't contain enough of them to have any measurable effect. Companies like Red Bull and Monster include them for marketing purposes to sound more interesting than coffee.[42]

Stop drinking those energy drinks, Christopher, they're full of sugar and crap.

Energy drinks also avoid the FDA's scrutiny by branding themselves as "dietary supplements"; that way they don't have to display caffeine contents or warnings. India's equivalent of the FDA wasn't a fan of this blatant duping, so in 2015, they banned Monster from the country entirely.[43]

Thankfully for yours truly, energy shots are a lot more innocent. 5-Hour Energy (and the Costco-branded knockoffs I drink, which I call my "Costcocaine") contains Vitamins B6 and B12 as primary ingredients, which stimulate cellular metabolism and neurotransmitter activity. Per my grandpa's words, the body just excretes what vitamins it doesn't use. The "no crash later" slogan, however, is misleading. If you read the fine print, you'll see that they mean no *sugar* crash—you'll still crash from the nearly 200 mg. of caffeine inside, roughly equivalent to a cup of coffee.

Caffeine is a great pleasure to consistently rely on for a good time, as it provides the energy and stamina to help us pursue a true happiness-building lifestyle. Ditch the sugary energy drinks and let the world's favorite beverage, coffee, give you wings instead.

Alcohol: The Science of Social Lube

Alcohol may be man's worst enemy, but the Bible says love your enemy.

—Frank Sinatra

Oh, alcohol. You're like the worst best friend I've ever had. You relaxed with me on a Mexican beach but forced my friend to drive off the road. You helped everyone have a good time at my stepbrother's wedding, then the next week you sent my friend's girlfriend to rehab.

Each time I want to curse you out for the last time, I reminisce on the good times we've had together and invite you back into my life. You're an endearing asshole on par with Hank Moody or Don Draper; I want to be around you, but you can be a *real dick* to me and my friends sometimes. In your defense, though, it's our fault for abusing you. What we often forget to remember is that like a marshmallow, you can be enjoyed in small doses sans nausea or regret.

It surprised me to learn that 60 percent of Americans consume less than a single drink per week. Half of those 60 percent don't even drink at all. I myself have about three drinks per week, putting me somewhere in the seventy-fifth percentile of drinkers. In college, I had about a *shelf* of alcohol per week (to borrow Ron Swanson's unit of measurement). Back then I'd routinely drink my way past the ninetieth percentile during a single *pregame*.

While most of our country barely drinks, our generation alone drinks about half the wine and nearly 100 percent of the craft beer sold here.[44] So why did our generation become so drinking-obsessed?

Well, it could be because our general views on drinking in this country are pretty polarizing and confusing. For example, the

Washington Post ran a story on the surprising statistics above, grabbing attention with the kinda-judgmental "if you drink two glasses of wine per night, that would put you in the top 20 percent." Just months earlier, the *Post* also published a blog to the homepage titled, "How to Get the Most Buzz for Your Buck." Turns out, a handle of Odesse vodka provides the cheapest way to get wasted.[(45)] Thanks, *Washington Post*!

America's Longest Love/Hate Relationship

The bizarre history of our drinking culture may shed a little light on our modern fascination. We've equally adored and despised alcohol for nearly two hundred years, but before that there wasn't much booze bipartisanship in our country. Right from the start, the Puritans were actually hauling more beer than water on the *Mayflower*, and only stopped at Plymouth Rock because they ran out of the former. As we began to colonize, the governor of Virginia called for more of his subjects to pick up the brewing trade. Connecticut *required* each town to have a liquor store.

Our forefathers weren't swigging in celebration of their liberation from their overseers like college freshmen free from their parents. Rather, they consumed alcohol as a cheap painkiller, and more importantly, a diuretic to fend off disease. I really wish Ben Franklin *did* say something along the lines of his famous Internet misquote: "In wine there is wisdom; in beer there is freedom; in water there is bacteria." But at least he *did* say, "Beer is proof that God loves us and wants us to be happy."

The church, continuing its role as the Western world's moral compass, weighed in on the booming brewing industry in the New World, but not as harshly as you might expect. Christianity never outright banned alcohol consumption like Islam (given alcohol plays a role in Christian mass), but the church understandably condemned its *over*consumption. Increase Mathers, a famous colonial minister and early Harvard graduate, once stated, "The wine is from God, but the drunkard is from the Devil." Speaking of, my favorite beer in the world is a Belgian amber called Duvel, meaning "devil," because of its deceptively high alcohol content that turns you into the devil. But I digress. On the whole, alcohol didn't have many enemies back in our colonial days.

As we grew as a country, so did our bar menu. By the mid-1600s, we began importing molasses and cane sugar from the Caribbean to make rum. Our westward expansion brought an overabundance of corn, which we used to make whiskey. Vodka made a brief appearance on the market between world wars, but suffered a PR crisis during the Red Scare. **No true-blooded American wanted to be seen drinking a commie cocktail until 1962, when Sean Connery ordered James Bond's first onscreen "shaken, not stirred" vodka martini.** Sales of Smirnoff skyrocketed shortly thereafter.

Of course, as our nation matured, our nonchalant national attitude toward alcohol changed. In the early 1800s, prohibitionist movements took seed in nearly every state. Women's rights groups, religious advocates, and even nativists began blaming alcohol for societal woes such as domestic abuse, political corruption, crime, and gambling. Soon, booze had few friends left in the Stars and Stripes, and in 1920 we signed the 18th Amendment, banning the sale, production, importation, and transportation of alcohol. Thirteen years later, a newly elected Franklin D. Roosevelt, desperate for tax revenue during the throes of the Great Depression, chose to repeal Prohibition. After signing the documents, he famously stated, "I think this would be a good time for a beer."[46]

So part of why it became so easy to vilify alcohol was because we clearly stopped ordering it for its diuretic properties a long time ago. **The Dude doesn't make White Russians to kill his cholera, nor does Bridget Jones sip Chardonnay to fight typhoid. Unlike marijuana, alcohol will probably never be prescribed for a practical, medical benefit. We just drink it because it's fun and feels good.**

Alcohol eases social situations, provides variety, and facilitates a sense of camaraderie with our fellow man. More broadly, it just relaxes us and affords a temporary escape from our stressful lives.

Chris Butsch

So what's going on up there when we take a swig? Does booze act like rubbing alcohol for our minds, numbing our neural pains?

Drunken Monkeys and Neural Narrowing

A popular modern theory for why we love alcohol comes from the hilariously named Drunken Monkey Hypothesis. According to lead researcher Robert Dudley, primates evolved as fruit eaters in tropical climates, where ripening fruit gave off a whiff of ethanol, i.e., the potable form of alcohol. Over time, our arboreal ancestors grew an instinctual association between alcohol and their dominant food source. The hypothesis, then, is that we may have inherited their primal attraction to the smell and taste of ethanol.[47]

I'm not knocking Dr. Dudley's theory. **After all, "primal attraction" is really our only excuse for drinking Fireball when we *know* it tastes like Satan's mouthwash.** But since we've all figured out that drinking alcohol numbs our cognitive abilities and reduces our survivability, shouldn't we have evolved to *avoid* it? Why are we still attracted to it?

"We drink alcohol to reduce associations in our mind," says Dr. Jonathan Rowson of the Royal Society of Arts. Ethanol weakens the signals between neurons, suppressing our continuous and strenuous processing of the world. "Alcohol typically elevates mood because with fewer associations to bother us, we start living less in our heads, and more in the here and now."[48] In other words, when we drink, our stressors and nagging mental to-do list just shut up for a bit, and we get to thrive in the blissful ignorance of cognitive narrowing. **Neurologically speaking, drinking tells our brains, "Hold all of my calls," so we can put our feet up on our desk (or dance on it).**

So is temporary leave of our senses and suppressed inner demons causing our taboo-shattering behavior? Alcohol's proven to make us *feel* funny . . . does it really make us *act* funny, too?

Turns out that while the physiological effects of inebriation are undeniable, our behavior is largely determined by culture. British anthropologist Kate Fox explains, "In high doses, alcohol impairs our reaction times, muscle control, coordination, short-term memory, perceptual field, cognitive abilities, and ability to speak clearly. But it does not cause us to selectively break specific social rules." She continues by providing super British examples. "It does not cause us to say, 'Oi, what you lookin' at?' and start punching each other. Nor does it cause us to say, 'Hey babe, fancy a shag?' and start groping each other."[49]

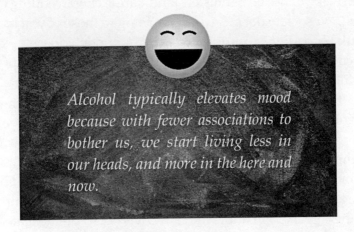

Alcohol typically elevates mood because with fewer associations to bother us, we start living less in our heads, and more in the here and now.

What she's saying is that alcohol doesn't make us act drunk; it makes us *think* we can act drunk. To test the theory that drunken behavior is largely conditioned, researchers in New Zealand conducted a devious experiment. They gave half of the partygoers at a crowded college pub potent vodka tonics while issuing the other half nonalcoholic versions of the same drink. Subjects were made aware of which version they'd received. Predictably, over the course of the evening the vodka-soaked group became more rowdy, jovial, and overconfident. The researchers then notified the entire pub that *nobody* had received alcohol that evening. The "drunk" group were simply *acting* drunk because they *thought* they were drunk.[50]

Essentially, when we drink to excess, we experience a paradigm shift in our thinking that tells us it's okay to begin acting drunk. Most of us can recall a time when a friend insisted, "I'm not drunk!"

and acted normal and collected shortly before tipping over into the grass. This is because he switched off his drunk *behavior*, but still succumbed to his physiological impediments, such as poor balance, slurred speech, and reduced cognition.

We only act ridiculous when we're drunk because, well, everyone else does. Then, the next morning nobody questions our unpredictable grab bag of personality changes. Instead, society widely accepts the idea that a single molecule causes us to flirt with our Uber drivers, dance on bannisters, and karate chop wedding cakes.

Well, *our* society does. As a fair warning to those of you looking to drink abroad, this conditioned "drunk mode" doesn't exist in every culture. The Italians associate drinking with meals and family time, and consider alcohol and disorder completely separate. One young Italian gang member reports, "When we go to fight, we do not drink—we want a clear mind." Likewise, the French consider drinking to be a social supplement, but not a key ingredient of a good time. Showing up to a French party with a case of beers may earn you weird glares and a *sacré bleu*. One student writes, "English people know before they go out if they are going to drink and how much they are likely to drink. In France, it is not so premeditated. We go out . . . sometimes we drink and sometimes we do not drink."[51]

I've taken a few paragraphs to expose "drunk mode" because I think it's the best way to reframe our personal relationships with alcohol for maximum gains to our own happiness. The anti-alcohol propaganda in the American education system is too binary; it loves to tell us, "When you drink, you *will* drive, get pregnant, and *die*," but the message falls on deaf ears because drinking is still fun. Plus, total dryness could actually be *bad* for us. A study published by the Society for the Study of Addiction revealed a U-shaped relationship between alcohol consumption and depression, meaning moderate drinkers are far less likely to report depression than heavy drinkers *and* nondrinkers alike.[52] **Complete personal prohibition is thought to cause social isolation and overstress, so in today's world, happy hour may actually be good for our happiness.**

So to stay in the middle of the curve, enjoy ourselves, and have a truly good time, we should adopt the drinking mindset followed by most of the world: when you're drinking, remember that you're still *you*, 100 percent, no excuses. Our "drunk mode" is just our own minds doing what we *think* we can get away with using alcohol as our scapegoat. Taking ownership of our actions while we drink is the first step in not only *feeling*, but *building* happiness with alcohol.

Maximizing Happiness: Finding Your Tipsy Prime

All right, so if we drink a bit, we'll give ourselves a nice neural massage and let our woes temporarily slip away. If we drink *too much*, we risk doing and saying things that we'll regret, waking up in jail, or worse, texting our ex. Is there a good stopping point where we stand to be the happiest? *What's the BAC of maximum joy?*

France, Italy, Greece, China, much of Latin America, and even Germany have what anthropologists call "integrated" drinking cultures, where alcohol laws are lax, drinking ages are young, and drinking itself is largely destigmatized. Drinking in these countries is a normal, healthy part of everyday life, and alcohol is poured at nearly every meal. You might think that wine-sipping integrated drinking cultures would drink less, but they actually drink even *more* than countries like England and America where abuse and alcoholism are prevalent.

The difference is that teenagers in these countries *learn* how to drink like we learn how to drive. Their families train them to find their comfortable limits, and instill in them that excess is taboo and unnecessary. My friend Franz's father began buying him beers in Germany when he was fourteen. "If ever I wanted a second, he'd tell me to wait a bit. Let it sink in. See how I was feeling. When I got older and had a few more, he would always politely tell me if he thought I'd had enough."

As adults, the people in these countries appreciate alcohol's ability to enhance a social situation, but hold each other accountable to retain their senses. They drink until they're relaxed but cognitively stable so they can continue to enjoy their surroundings. In essence, people in integrated drinking cultures have found the fulcrum where alcohol provides maximum pleasure *and* true happiness. They don't really have a name for it, so I call it the "tipsy prime."

The problem in America is that unlike most of the world, we often don't respect or even know where our tipsy prime is. Our culture has taught us to surge past it, oftentimes involuntarily; friends buy us another round, we're playing a drinking game, or we simply indulge the impulse to fill our empty Solo cup. The key, then, is to treat alcohol like food; intake it slowly so we can listen to our bodies' signals. There will come a time when we feel pretty chilled out, but still able to carry a normal conversation, and *that's* the best time to stop. After we've found our tipsy prime, we can maintain it by sipping about a drink per hour, or stopping drinking altogether.

Once you gain a sense for where your tipsy prime is, and can effectively drink to it a few times in a row, congratulations! You've joined hundreds of millions of the happiest drinkers in the world from Germany, China, Greece, Brazil, and other integrated drinking cultures. There's real beauty and pragmatism to the tipsy prime; you'll relax, save money, enjoy yourself, remember everything, make friends, have great conversations, and wake up with no hangover or need for damage control. Isn't that what you *really* want from a night out?

That being said, even once you've found your tipsy prime, there'll always be times when you'll be tempted to just chug past it—a friend's wedding, losing at the Oscars, etc. I'm sure you have the judgment to get home safe, but you're still wasted and highly vulnerable to a big ol' brain slap heading your way tomorrow morning.

So before we wrap up our happy drinking education, let's address one of happiness's oldest adversaries: the hangover.

Hangover Helper

I was certain my college roommate Clark would be hungover the next morning. Sober men aren't known to pee into mini fridges. But I was so blitzed myself, I knew I faced a similar fate. Recollecting the common belief that hangovers are caused by dehydration, I took solace in remembering that I had a lemonade-flavored Vitaminwater waiting for me in the fridge. But I was already in bed . . . plus, it probably had Clark's homemade lemonade on it now.

The next morning, we filled our dorm with a sad duet of groaning and profanity. *I'm never drinking again*, I thought for the fourth time that semester. Clark spoke the first full sentence of the morning: "I think you left a Vitaminwater in the bathroom."

The Vitaminwater, which Clark graciously rinsed off for me, helped a ton. But dehydration isn't the cause of a hangover; it's just a side effect. If you've ever had a friend lament, "Ugh, my liver is going to kill me tomorrow," she was spot on.

A hangover begins with the basic digestive process. As you finish dinner, your stomach breaks down your burger, salad, and beer into particles small enough for your liver to process. Enzymes in the liver then sort out the nutrients from the toxins, so the good stuff can be absorbed into the bloodstream and the garbage can be flushed out.

When the enzymes encounter ethanol, they condense it into a highly toxic form called acetaldehyde, essentially packaging it for efficient flushing out of the body. Then, a *specialized* enzyme called glutathione swoops in to eject it from the body.

But we only have so much glutathione, and when we keep drinking all night, it just can't process the acetaldehyde fast enough; the conveyor belt is just going too fast. So the super-dense, super-toxic version of alcohol ends up flowing into our bloodstream with our nutrients, resulting in headaches, nausea, and dizziness the next morning. The hangover subsides when our glutathione catches up and successfully flushes the acetaldehyde out of our system.

So why hasn't anyone invented a glutathione shake to sell at the bar? Good question—if you're a chemical engineer, look into it for all of us!

In the meantime, we can prevent and treat hangovers in a few ways. Obviously, the best way is to stick to our tipsy prime. But if you just have to rage, alternate drinks with water: beer, water, wine, water, tequila shot, water, etc. This will help your body process the alcohol more efficiently and keep your brain hydrated, preventing the headache. The next morning, eggs, bananas, and fruit juice all contain chemicals that accelerate the acetaldehyde-disposal process.

In summary, alcohol can be a cruel jerk to us. But by sticking with our tipsy prime we can *use* alcohol as a way to relax, expand our comfort zones, and continue building happiness through new friendships and memories. By practicing tactile moderation, we'll relax but retain our vital cognition, enabling us to have a truly good time.

Marijuana: The Changing Face of Ganja

"Whatever you do, don't tell Chris," said my neighbor Craig to my friend Matt. He then passed my friend a freshly packed bowl of the dankest weed he'd ever smoked.

The night before, Matt had arrived in Wanee for the music festival and set up camp with a cohort of flannel-touting friends. The next morning, he unzipped his tent and pulled up a folding chair over to the nearest communal campfire, joining a mix of familiar and unfamiliar faces. Through the smoke, only some of which was from the campfire, he locked eyes with my former babysitter and Boy Scout leader. They stared at each other with bloodshot eyes.

"Matt?"

"*Craig?*"

The jig was up, because in Matt's words, "You don't go to Wanee unless you smoke weed." Finding a nontoker at Wanee would be like finding a library card in a Kardashian's purse. So the *last* person Matt thought he'd see was my pious neighbor Craig, a living Ned Flanders who drove a wood-paneled station wagon and could find a way to bring up Jesus in a conversation about sandwiches.

Matt and Craig, who'd bumped into each other a few times before at my house, smoked together all weekend. Matt also kept his promise of discretion, and I was none the wiser about his Wanee adventure. Months later, I'd convinced Craig to have a few beers with me on my porch, and after a few high-proof scotch ales, he opened up. "Chris, you're twenty-four . . . can we talk about weed now?"

Craig confessing his smoking habit to me was like debunking Santa Clause to a forty-three-year-old. I had known for years, and struggled to hold back giggles like a shaken champagne bottle. The evidence was everywhere; when I babysat his kids in high school, Craig would return home and hang his sweater vests outside, coming in through the back door. He avidly collected folk art and attended music festivals. His favorite store was called Terrapin Station, the marquee for which featured a visibly stoned turtle riding a locomotive. His Spotify recommendations could add appropriate ambiance to a Colorado dispensary, replete with Willie Nelson, The Grateful Dead, Phish, and Dave Matthews.

From the day I put the pieces together about a decade prior, I didn't care. I think he might've been worried I'd think less of him or judge him, but far from it. He's a high-performing, well-respected CEO of his own company—the guy deserves a little break.

Craig's reluctance to admit to a casual smoking habit is testament to our systemic stigmatization of marijuana in this country. **How can a widely enjoyed drug with no recorded overdoses be so viciously vilified? Bong-ripping conspiracy theorists will tell you, "It's the government, MAN!" Turns out, they're exactly right.**

Had I learned everything I knew about pot from the Drug Enforcement Agency's website, I'd be terrified for Craig's life. The DEA still classifies marijuana as a Schedule I Controlled Substance "with no currently accepted medical use in the United States."[53] This designation has led to hilariously misguided assertions that pot is equally as dangerous as other Schedule I substances like heroin or ecstasy, and even worse than Schedule II substances like crystal meth. Growing up, D.A.R.E. told us weed was "a gateway drug."

To test their theory, let's take a quiz. You and your friends are sitting around, each as high as Cheech and Chong combined. How is this sentence most likely to end?

"Hey man, would you be down for some _____?"

a) Heroin
b) Crack Cocaine
c) Crystal Meth
d) Taco Bell

Yes, the correct answer is (d), and Mark Kleiman, a UCLA researcher, would agree. Known as the "pot czar," Dr. Kleiman is a marijuana consultant to Washington who says that weed isn't so much a gateway to other drugs as it is to illegal activity in general. "It can get them into illicit drugs because it gets them to know people who sell illicit drugs," and as pro-legalization pundits note, this is further reason to legalize it.[54]

And trends are moving that way. At the time of this writing, recreational marijuana is legal in Alaska, Colorado, Oregon, Washington, and DC, with a further eighteen states having decriminalized it or legalized it for "medical" purposes.

To explain the quotes, it's not hard to get a medical marijuana prescription—in California at least, where one journalist timed himself to go from out-of-townie to legally stoned local. To accrue his legal pot, he'd have to get a California driver's license, visit a doctor to get approved for a prescription, and visit a dispensary to make a purchase. His time? Two hours and forty-seven minutes, including a long wait at the DMV.[55]

So once you arrive in Cali, you could get legally baked before the end of *Lord of the Rings*. But if you're like me, you have a handful of good friends who will just share with you. My friend Ryan smoked me up before we saw *Mad Max: Fury Road*, which turned out to be a stupendously good decision. Despite the bodacious effect being high had on my narrative transport, I rarely think about weed, nor have I ever bought any. Marijuana to me is like

Six Flags. On any given day, I have no desire to go to Six Flags. But when my friends show up with a ticket, *best day ever.*

So how do we as a generation feel about weed as a whole? Legalize or condemn?

Reliable statistics about our generation's smoking habits are hard to come by, since we're apparently too stoned to finish surveys. In Fusion's Massive Millennial Poll, when asked whether we'd ever smoked pot, 1 percent of us answered "I don't know."[56] I'd love to read the follow-ups to those answers, like *I don't know, I got a buzz making out with a guy at Burning Man, does that count?*

The Pew Research Center finally managed to pull *something* useful out of us: the fact that 68 percent of our generation approves of legalization.[37] Two-thirds of 84 million is a powerful voting voice, so it could be our generation that turns our country green.

But is our marijuana consumption a good thing? Sure, getting a little high makes Cheetos, South Park, and sex much better, but as with the abuse of other drugs, are we on the losing side of a neurological tradeoff?

Hemp History

Humans have been using cannabis for millennia for its wide range of perceived benefits. The Vikings used it to dull toothaches. Indians used it to relieve anxiety. The ancient Chinese used it to cure "the female weakness" (why they thought getting grandma baked would help is a mystery).[57]

Plus, surely everybody consumed marijuana because it releases dopamine and makes us happy, perhaps more so than many other pleasures in its price range.

So the human race has been smoking it for millennia, and our generation strongly approves of seeing dispensaries on every corner. Doctors give it to our grandparents to relieve chronic pain, and we smoke it to pregame 3-D movies. Weed seems like a win-win for all involved; so when and how did it get such a bad reputation?

"The idea that [marijuana] is an evil drug is a very recent construction," says Professor Barney Warf, author of *High Points: A Historical Geography of Cannabis.* In his report, he outlines how Americans actually weren't a part of the worldwide toke-fest until 1910, when Mexican immigrants brought Mary Jane across the border.

Predictably, the immigrants were unwelcomed, and despite their docility were quickly blamed for criminal activity around the border states. When lawmen discovered marijuana during raids in Mexican neighborhoods, they were quick to condemn it. "Many early prejudices against marijuana were thinly veiled racist fears of its smokers, often promulgated by reactionary newspapers," says Warf.[58]

The drug was slowly banned at the state level, and in 1937 we banned it altogether, placing regulation under the DEA's jurisdiction. In 1970, following the advice of the assistant secretary of health, Congress assigned a temporary Schedule I status to marijuana, noting the "considerable void in our knowledge of the plant and effects."[59]

It's hard to blame our government for telling us not to smoke a psychotropic drug we knew nothing about. Two years of research later, the National Commission on Marijuana and Drug Abuse made the official recommendation to Congress that we decriminalize marijuana at a federal level. Perhaps distracted by the smell of napalm, the Nixon administration ignored the recommendation, and marijuana has been stuck in Schedule I status ever since, imprisoned for a crime it never actually committed.

Nowadays, marijuana research is notoriously difficult to do right. As a Schedule I substance, marijuana is still classified as more dangerous than cocaine and even crystal meth, so clinical research requires a license from the DEA *and* approval from the FDA. Once you have those, just *getting* research-grade marijuana requires wading through a sea of forms from the National Institute for Drug Abuse. Over the past few years, however, we've learned a few things from researchers who have either cut through the red tape or gone off the books.

Ganja Science

Cannabis contains around sixty types of cannabinoids, or chemical compounds that interact with our neurological receptors to cause a grab bag of effects. Their ringleader is tetrahydrocannabinol, or THC, which resembles another chemical in our brains regulating mood, sleep, memory, and appetite. The other cannabinoids relieve pain, lower anxiety, and most importantly for our happiness, release dopamine.

But due to the difficulty of conducting research, longitudinal studies of marijuana's *long*-term impacts on our brain are scant and mostly inconclusive thus far. We have learned that cannabinoids have been known to trigger schizophrenia or heightened anxiety, so put down the bong if those run in the family.

The most credible drawback we've discovered is how smoking it affects our respiratory system. Weed smoke contains more carcinogens than unfiltered tobacco smoke, which is known to break down the tissue of our lungs. Though longitudinal studies exist both proving and disproving marijuana smoke's link to lung cancer, it's safe to say it's probably not doing us any favors.

To summarize, weed was initially outlawed due to racism, stayed temporarily illegal due to caution, and remains mostly illegal today due to bureaucratic inertia. Though scant, research generally asserts that it's been wrongfully damned for the past century. Weed isn't killing us, nor has it proven itself a menace to society as we were raised to believe. But perhaps the greatest con to good ol' Mary Jane isn't her physiological drawbacks, since we haven't really found any, or her bad reputation. The greatest con to weed's existence, if there is one, might just be how *well it works*.

To illustrate, let's look at the lazy stoner stereotype. Why do pathological weed-smokers typically seem less driven, with a penchant for Dominos delivery and *Futurama* marathons? Weed provides an instant release of dopamine, without the debilitating after-effects of alcohol or cocaine. To some, this access to cheap, on-demand happiness lessens their drive to venture into the real world and invest in their long-term happiness.

"I used marijuana as a way to run from my problems as opposed to facing them," my friend Spencer, twenty-five, told me. "Getting high every day was something I wish I could've done differently. I missed out on so many things: friends, family, overall bettering myself. Marijuana, like many things, can easily get out of hand when we start to associate happiness with certain actions." Since shifting from a habitual to casual smoker, Spencer has begun pursuing a career as a professional editor, and has even glanced over this very section.

Hazing our aspirations isn't Mary Jane's only fault; weed simply hasn't harmonized with our society yet. Socially, weed often divides the smokers from the nonsmokers, the latter often disquieted by its illegal status. Calling our weed-loving friends "stoners," even if we do so without venom, may be giving them an unfair, derogatory label, perpetuating their habit. In their defense, they're usually not as dangerous or self-harming as alcoholics, but their smoking habits similarly impede their mindfulness and pursuit of passions.

Getting high every day was something I wish I could've done differently. I missed out on so many things: friends, family, overall bettering myself. Marijuana, like many things, can easily get out of hand when we start to associate happiness with certain actions.

I'm certainly not condemning weed. In fact, Craig and I occasionally enjoy some CEO-grade dank-ass grass together. Like many pleasures, weed can nicely supplement a life of true happiness, and in social scenarios, help build it. Just don't become seduced by its dopamine-releasing properties and let it inhibit your motivation and hunger for personal growth. Also, given we haven't turned the country green *yet*, toke with tacted and keep your employer's rules and local laws in mind.

Cocaine: A Helluva Drug

"Have you ever tried cocaine?" I asked.

"Yeah, exactly twice."

My best friend Jamie and I were cruising down a Nashville turnpike, on our way to a speaking engagement at a local high school. I've never tried hard drugs, despite always having them figuratively at arm's reach in college and from colleagues at work. I wasn't adhering to some strict personal dogma; they'd just never interested me, like Zumba or watching hockey. Programs like D.A.R.E. in high school had flat out lied about marijuana usage, so I'd always wondered if cocaine was as life-ending as we were told.

What Jamie told me next would settle my mind.

"Why twice?"

"Well, I tried it once after high school graduation, and it felt pretty incredible."

"And?"

"I tried it again a week later, and it just didn't feel as good. I knew to reach that first high, I'd have to do more each time. It scared the hell out of me."

I'm so grateful that my best friend stopped doing cocaine quickly, because had he not, he wouldn't be the same person today. Before I try my best to deter you from ever burying your face in booger sugar, let's build some context.

Cocaine is an alkaloid, or plant-based compound with a known physiological effect on humans. It comes from the South American

Erythroxylom coca plant, one that indigenous tribes have been chewing for thousands of years. When the Spanish arrived, they immediately went nuts for the nutrient-rich and energizing plant, and began exporting it.

By the mid-1800s, advances in chemistry enabled European scientists to isolate the cocaine alkaloid from the coca leaf. In 1879, a German scientist tested cocaine's stimulating abilities by immersing frog legs in a cocaine-treated solution. Noting the increased activity, he concluded that the civilized world had finally discovered a drug to help white men dance.

For the rest of the nineteenth century, cocaine made its way into medicine cabinets, tonics, foods, and even wine. In 1886, a former Confederate officer created a tasty brain tonic by adding a pinch of cocaine to each serving. Searching for a catchy, alliterative name, he landed on Coca-Cola.

But like alcohol, cocaine eventually fell out of America's good graces. In the early 1900s, the powers that be linked cocaine usage to increased violence, prostitution, and murder among the lower class. States gradually introduced cocaine-banning legislature, and the Harrison Narcotics Tax Act of 1914 relegated cocaine to behind the pharmacy counter. In 1922, it was banned altogether, and has been since.

So how exactly did cocaine get so popular? By making us extremely happy, for an extremely short amount of time, at extreme cost. Cocaine acts by flooding our dopamine receptors with five to ten times the normal dopamine we usually feel when we're having a good time. As a result, we enjoy an unprecedented jolt in pleasure, energy, and motivation. The effect lasts around fifteen to thirty minutes, then we fall down from cloud nine.

Doesn't sound so bad, but here's the big problem: we've spent a lifetime carefully calibrating our brains' reward system. Our brains know a pumpkin-spice latte tastes *this* good, and a first kiss feels *that* good. Cocaine comes in and karate kicks those scales over, and in the words of neuroscientist Adam Kepecs, "hijacks" those systems.[59] Our brain quickly realizes that nothing else can make us as happy as cocaine (not even *five* pumpkin-spice lattes), and demands for us to get more. Per Jamie's story, the next time we do it, we need more to achieve the levels brought on by that first high. But regardless of whether we achieve a better high, we're never *satisfied*. That's when addiction sets in.

It gets worse, because as cocaine supersoaks us with dopamine, our receptors become numb and eventually shut off altogether. Since those receptors never grow back, we actually *lose our capacity for happiness*.

So cocaine is like a friend who gives you $100,000. Whoa, it feels *amazing* to have a hundred grand! But fifteen minutes later, he demands it all back. Plus, he'll also make sure you *never* make $100,000 in your life, so if you ever want to make that much money again, you have to get it from him.

I say screw him; let's go make our own money.

Crack, Heroin, Meth, Etc.: Seriously, Not Even Once

Hopefully most of us reading this aren't considering doing anything life-ruining like heroin or crystal meth. Consider that these drugs are so vile, not even Hollywood or hardcore gangsta rap ever tries to glamorize them.

While I still lived up north, my friend Mallory worked in the ER as part of her residency. My apartment was between hers and the hospital, so she'd often drop by after her shift for a beer to decompress. On more than one occasion she knocked on my door in tears. One night she told me, "I watched too many kids die tonight."

During that particular shift she'd seen sixteen young people come in for heroin overdoses; four of them died. She half-heartedly assured me that the docs usually save more of them, but she continued to see dozens of OD-related admissions every weekend. She'd pray that the survivors would seek help and kick the habit.

Heroin is responsible for the premature deaths of Coco Chanel, Janis Joplin, Jim Morrison, Philip Seymour Hoffman, and my favorite comedian, Mitch Hedberg. For many I spoke with, it took their brother, sister, or best friend.

Are these people simply outliers, or is heroin really that addictive and lethal? To find out, one Reddit user created a blog where he tried every popular recreational drug to compare and contrast their effects. In a few weeks he'd tried cocaine, Adderall, nitrous oxide, Xanax, and a few others. Feeling safe behind the walls of a nonaddictive personality, he then tried heroin just once. Two weeks later, he posted again, begging for help. "Heroin pretty much f***ed my life for me in two weeks, I just want to die." Then, he went silent. Four years later, he posted again, admitting to a failed suicide attempt after trying to go sober. He kicked his heroin habit only after a year and a half of rehab.

Another Reddit user reports being a semifunctional user of heroin, but he's far from content. He describes heroin use as a new basic need, like food or shelter. **"Imagine your belly is full of expensive food . . . or you're surrounded by love and comfort . . . or falling asleep in the arms of the girl of your dreams. You're still lacking."**

Meth is even scarier. A former meth addict I spoke with started life as a straight-A student. After he and his best friend Theo tried meth once, he lost motivation for everything in life except getting high. He worked in a warehouse, making just enough to get high and meet his basic needs every day. Three years later he was sharing a pipe in an abandoned trailer with four other junkies: his only friends. Capitalizing on a rare moment of clarity, he decided to get clean. Seven months later, someone broke into his house and stole everything of value he owned. He later found out it was Theo, but before he could find his old friend and help him kick his addiction, Theo hanged himself.

The lesson here is that trying these drugs sentences you to a fate arguably worse than death; they reduce and even permanently disable your capacity for true happiness. Perhaps we could overcome drug use altogether if dealers opened with a single, honest disclaimer: "Try this, then everything that makes you happy won't ever work as well again."

The Rock Star Lifestyle: A Highway to Hell

Addictive activities produce momentary pleasure but long-term misery and regret.
— Professor John Robinson, lead researcher
of the thirty-year General Social Survey

Now's a good time to reiterate that safe (and legal) pleasures are an important part of life. If we bake a cake of true happiness, pleasures will be the icing. In a pinch, they can provide a happiness boost we need to get through the day. The critical takeaway is that pleasures should *supplement* happiness, not be its sole source. If we live our lives hopping from pleasure to pleasure without investing in true happiness, we're living what some positive psychologists call the Rock Star Lifestyle. It feels good jumping from pleasure high to pleasure high, but under the surface, our true happiness is atrophying like an untrained muscle. This is how depression sneaks up on the famous and prosperous, and it's precisely what happened to me.

While I was still at my first job, my friends eventually gave up trying to make plans with me during the week. Within a few months of starting work, I began staying at the office later and later, desperately trying not to drown in a sea of emails. Soon the cleaning crews and I greeted each other by name as I headed to the vending machine for a subsidized can of Monster.

Even on days when I could escape the office early for a friend's birthday or a date, I wasn't much company; I had spent all of my mental energy at the office, so my mind was like a fast car with an ounce of fuel, soon sputtering to an undignified halt. After 8 p.m., I was a husk, eyes half open, Yelping for nearby takeout or a drive-thru to end the day with a cheap pleasure high from food. In short, I felt ego depleted *every single day*.

Since I felt constant ego depletion, I had neither the time nor energy to build true happiness, so I got a fix from pleasures instead. On the half-hour drives home I'd blast music and speed to feel a cheap thrill. At stoplights, I'd flip rapid-fire through Reddit, Facebook, and StumbleUpon content on my phone. I often felt I deserved junk food for dinner, and would play video games for hours to numb myself. On weekends, I'd drink too much and go out with my guy friends to seek out casual sexual encounters (thankfully with tempered results). For a while I even read up on pickup-artist techniques. *Ugh.*

I had a wonderful group of friends by this point, but didn't spend nearly enough time with them. I stopped reading nonfiction like I used to, and lost touch with high school and college friends. I was working almost nonstop, including Sundays. **Adult life is a marathon and I was sprinting the first mile, telling myself I could eventually slow down.** But my hedonic set point was dropping; soon, I needed pleasures like I needed oxygen.

I had lived the Rock Star Lifestyle for over a year, letting my true happiness wilt like a neglected office plant. My life was almost entirely devoid of long-term happiness, so I needed more and more pleasures to feel the same temporary "highs." I'd get larger sodas at the drive-thru, play video games longer, sleep in, drink more caffeine. The time I spent between pleasures felt worse and worse, until eventually, I became depressed.

Depression, then, was like having my car break down. Pleasures were like pushing it forward, whereas building true happiness was like repairing the engine. In the former case, I was getting exhausted and hardly getting anywhere. True happiness may not have had the instant gratification of movement, but eventually got the whole vehicle moving again.

Through my research for this book, I've noticed that the Rock Star Lifestyle is the culprit for much of our generation's misery.

We have access to more wealth and pleasures than anyone else on the planet, and as a result we tend to gravitate toward these pleasures before we discover the power of true happiness. I had a well-paying job, a loving family, and caring friends when I was diagnosed with clinical depression. I learned the hard way that the Rock Star Lifestyle is a highway to hell, one that we can stay off of by realizing when we've begun indulging in too many pleasures and lost sight of what makes us truly happy.

The Tipping Point

Somewhere in *your* journey to happiness, you'll reach a critical moment when you start preferring to build true happiness over indulging in pleasures. You'd rather go out with friends than stay home and play the newest video game. You'd rather meditate and read than get stoned and watch mindless TV. Not every time, but most times. Your mind will have internalized the power of investing in true happiness and personal growth over the instant gratification of pleasures.

Building true happiness is a lot like going to the gym; you go from *not* doing it, to doing it because you know you *should*, to doing it because you *want* to. And the day when you start preferring true happiness over pleasures is the beginning of the rest of your life. The remaining chapters of this book are written to help you find and stay on the path. Your mind, body, and wallet will thank you.

So now that we're waving bon voyage to Pleasure Island, let's set sail for the happy mainland. Our first step is to build a vehicle to get there.

References:

1) Huta, Veronika, and Alan S. Waterman. "Eudaimonia and its distinction from hedonia: Developing a classification and terminology for understanding conceptual and operational definitions." *Journal of Happiness Studies* 15, no. 6 (2014): 1425–1456.

2) Paul, Margaret. "Happiness Versus Pleasure." December 31, 2006. Accessed January 19, 2015. http://www.innerbonding.com/show-article/652/happiness-versus-pleasure.html.

3) "TV and Video Revenue Worldwide in 2015 and 2020 (in Billion U.S. Dollars)." 2015. Accessed March 20, 2016. https://www.statista.com/statistics/259985/global-filmed-entertainment-revenue/.

4) "Fast Food Still Major Part of U.S. Diet." August 6, 2013. Accessed March 20, 2016. http://www.gallup.com/poll/163868/fast-food-major-part-diet.aspx.

5) "Chipotle Investor Relations - Press Release." February 02, 2016. Accessed May 16, 2016. http://ir.chipotle.com/phoenix.zhtml?c=194775&p=irol-newsArticle&ID=2134993.

6) Tuttle, Brad. "10 Things Millennials Buy Far More Often Than Everyone Else." July 31, 2015. Accessed February 24, 2016. http://time.com/money/3979425/Millennials-consumers-boomers-gen-x/.

7) Edwards, Stephen. "Instant Gratification Is the Downfall of Generation Y." July 28, 2015. Accessed February 24, 2016. http://elitedaily.com/money/entrepreneurship/instant-gratification-downfall-generation/.

8) Eyal, Nir. *Hooked: How to Build Habit-Forming Products.* London, United Kingdom: Portfolio Penguin, 2014.

9) McCluskey, Megan. "Instagram Star Essena O'Neill Breaks Her Silence on Quitting Social Media." January 5, 2016. Accessed December 30, 2015. http://time.com/4167856/essena-oneill-breaks-silence-on-quitting-social-media/.

10) Parsons, Jeff. "2 out of Every 3 People Admit to Doing This on Facebook to Seem More Adventurous." *Technology.* October 16, 2015. Posted February 20, 2016. http://www.mirror.co.uk/news/technology-science/technology/study-reveals-almost-everybody-lies-6644960.

11) Clayton, Russell B., Alexander Nagurney, and Jessica R. Smith. "Cheating, Breakup, and Divorce: Is Facebook Use to Blame?" *Cyberpsychology, Behavior, and Social Networking* 16, no. 10 (October 2013): 717–20.

12) Andsberg, Kjartan, Marie Lundby, Morten Trumholt, and Meik Weiking. "The Facebook Experiment: Does Social Media Affect the Quality of Our Lives?" *Happiness Research Institute* 2015. http://www.happinessresearchinstitute.com/download/i/mark_dl/u/4012182887/4624845731/The%20Facebook%20Experiment.pdf.

13) Gearhardt, Ashley N., Carlos M. Grilo, Ralph J. DiLeone, Kelly D. Brownell, and Marc N. Potenza. "Can Food Be Addictive? Public Health and Policy Implications." *Addiction* 106, no. 7 (February 14, 2011): 1208–12. doi:10.1111/j.1360-0443.2010.03301.x.

14) Lenoir, Magalie, Fuschia Serre, Lauriane Cantin, and Serge H. Ahmed. "Intense Sweetness Surpasses Cocaine Reward." Edited by Bernhard Baune. *PLoS ONE* 2, no. 8 (August 1, 2007): e698. doi:10.1371/journal.pone.0000698.

15) Moss, Michael S. *Salt, Sugar, Fat: How the Food Giants Hooked Us.* New York: Random House Publishing Group, 2013.

16) Rolls, Barbara J. "Sensory-Specific Satiety." *Nutrition Reviews* 44, no. 3 (April 27, 2009): 93–101. doi:10.1111/j.1753-4887.1986.tb07593.x.

17) Witherly, Steven Anthony. *Why Humans Like Junk Food*. iUniverse, 2007.

18) Turow, Eve. "A Taste of Generation Yum: How the Millennial Generation's Love for Organic Fare, Celebrity Chefs and Microbrews Will Make or Break the Future of Food." July 1, 2015. Accessed February 23, 2016.

19) Kapleau, Philip. *The Three Pillars of Zen: Teaching, Practice, and Enlightenment*. 25th ed. New York: Knopf Doubleday Publishing Group, 1989.

20) Wolever, Ruth, Beth Reardon, Tania Hannan, and Beth Reardon MS Rd Ldn. *The Mindful Diet: How to Transform Your Relationship with Food for Lasting Weight Loss and Vibrant Health*. Philadelphia, PA, United States: Simon & Schuster Children's Publishing, 2014.

21) "Essential Facts about the Computer and Video Game Industry." April 2015. Accessed March 14, 2016. http://www.theesa.com/wp-content/uploads/2015/04/ESA-Essential-Facts-2015.pdf.

22) Kim, Eugene. "Amazon Buys Twitch for $970 Million in Cash." August 25, 2014. Accessed March 15, 2016. http://www.businessinsider.com/amazon-buys-twitch-2014-8.

23) Bavelier, Daphne. *Your Brain on Video Games*. November 19, 2012. Posted March 16, 2016. https://www.ted.com/talks/daphne_bavelier_your_brain_on_video_games?language=en.

24) Wright, Will. "Transcript of 'Spore, birth of a game.'" July 2007. Accessed September 20, 2016. https://www.ted.com/talks/will_wright_makes_toys_that_make_worlds/transcript?language=en.

25) Chatfield, Tom. "Transcript of '7 ways games reward the brain.'" November 2010. Accessed September 20, 2016.

https://www.ted.com/talks/tom_chatfield_7_ways_ga mes_reward_the_brain/transcript?language=en#t-655000.

26) Brown, Stuart, Christopher Vaughan, and M. Stuart, D. Brown. *Play: How It Shapes the Brain, Opens the Imagination, and Invigorates the Soul*. New York: Avery Publishing Group, 2009.

27) Herodotus, "Herodotus on Lydia," *Ancient History Encyclopedia*, last modified January 18, 2012, http://www.ancient.eu/article/81/.

28) Cook, James. "REVEALED: Elon Musk's Favourite Video Games." January 6, 2015. Accessed March 20, 2016. http://www.businessinsider.com/elon-musks-favourite-video-games-2015-1?r=UK&IR=T.

29) Mueller, Saira. "Mark Cuban Might Be Getting into Esports, Plays *League of Legends* Showmatch at IEM San Jose." December 11, 2015. Accessed March 20, 2016. http://www.dailydot.com/esports/mark-cuban-esports-league-of-legends-iem-san-jose/.

30) Yahr, Emily. "How Much TV Do Millennials Watch a Day? Depends on What Kind of Millennial You Are." *Washington Post* (Washington Post), March 24, 2016. https://www.washingtonpost.com/news/arts-and-entertainment/wp/2016/03/24/how-much-tv-do-Millennials-watch-a-day-depends-on-what-kind-of-Millennial-you-are/.

31) Lipsman, Andrew. "The U.S. Total Video Report." October 14, 2014. Accessed October 16, 2016. http://www.comscore.com/Insights/Presentations-and-Whitepapers/2014/The-US-Total-Video-Report.

32) Reinecke, Leonard, Tilo Hartmann, and Allison Eden. "The Guilty Couch Potato: The Role of Ego Depletion in Reducing Recovery Through Media Use." *Journal of Communication* 64, no. 4 (June 24, 2014): 569–89. doi:10.1111/jcom.12107.

33) Hanna, Heidi. *Stressaholic: 5 Steps to Transform Your Relationship with Stress*. United States: Wiley & Sons Canada, Limited, John, 2014.

34) Stromberg, Peter G. "Why Is Entertainment so Entertaining?" 1991. Accessed March 20, 2016. https://www.psychologytoday.com/blog/sex-drugs-and-boredom/200908/why-is-entertainment-so-entertaining.

35) Conlin, Lindsey and Adam Sharples. "Binge-Watching: Transportation into Narrative TV Content." August 6, 2014. Accessed September 20, 2016. http://citation.allacademic.com/meta/p_mla_apa_rese arch_citation/7/2/8/7/5/p728758_index.html.

36) Oliver, Mary Beth and Anne Bartsch. "Appreciation as Audience Response: Exploring Entertainment Gratifications Beyond Hedonism." *Human Communication Research* 36, no. 1 (January 2010): 53–81. doi:10.1111/j.1468-2958.2009.01368.x.

37) Motel, Seth. "6 Facts About Marijuana." April 14, 2015. Accessed March 21, 2016. http://www.pewresearch.org/fact-tank/2015/04/14/6-facts-about-marijuana/.

38) Schumaker, Erin. "Just How Dangerous Are Energy Drinks, Anyway?" *The Huffington Post*, June 23, 2014. http://www.huffingtonpost.com/2014/06/23/just-how-dangerous-are-energy-drinks_n_5515647.html.

39) "Update on Caffeinated Alcoholic Beverages." June 16, 2013. Accessed March 21, 2016. http://www.fda.gov/NewsEvents/PublicHealthFocus/ucm234900.htm.

40) "Millennials: An Important Segment for Coffee Consumption, Proexport Says." September 2016. Accessed September 21, 2016. http://www.cafedecolombia.com/bb-fnc-en/index.php/comments/Millennials_an_important_s egment_for_coffee_consumption_proexport_says.

41) Seroka, Rachel and Angela Babb. "Hold the Diet Soda? Sweetened Drinks Linked to Depression, Coffee May Lower Risk." January 12, 2013. Accessed March 21, 2016. https://www.aan.com/PressRoom/home/GetDigitalA sset/10430.

42) Higgins, John P., Troy D. Tuttle, and Christopher L. Higgins. "Energy Beverages: Content and Safety." *Mayo Clinic Proceedings* 85, no. 11 (November 1, 2010). Accessed March 21, 2016. http://www.ncbi.nlm.nih.gov/pmc/articles/PMC2966367/.

43) Stanford, Duane D. *Monster Fights to Stay in India After Its Drinks Are Banned*. Bloomberg. June 26, 2015. http://www.bloomberg.com/news/articles/2015-06-26/monster-fights-to-stay-in-india-after-its-drinks-are-banned.

44) Fromm, Jeff. "The Millennial Consumer Craves Craft Beer." *Millennial Marketing*. January 2014. http://www.Millennialmarketing.com/2014/01/the-Millennial-consumer-craves-craft-beer/.

45) Ingraham, Christopher. "The Beverage Curve: How to Get the Most Buzz for Your Buck." *Washington Post* (Washington Post), May 23, 2014. https://www.washingtonpost.com/news/wonk/wp/2014/05/23/the-beverage-curve-how-to-get-the-most-buzz-for-your-buck/.

46) Friedrich, Otto. "F.D.R.'S Disputed Legacy." February 1, 1982. Accessed March 21, 2016. http://content.time.com/time/magazine/article/0,9171,954983-6,00.html.

47) Dudley, R. (2014). *The Drunken Monkey: Why We Drink and Abuse Alcohol*. Berkeley: University of California Press. 154 pp.

48) Rowson, Jonathan. "Seriously, Why Do We Drink Alcohol? - RSA." February 21, 2012. Accessed March 21, 2016. https://www.thersa.org/discover/publications-

and-articles/rsa-blogs/2012/02/seriously-why-do-we-drink-alcohol.

49) BBC. "Viewpoint: Is the Alcohol Message All Wrong?" *BBC Magazine* (BBC News), October 12, 2011. http://www.bbc.com/news/magazine-15265317.

50) Assefi, Seema L. and Maryanne Garry. "Absolut® Memory Distortions." *Psychological Science* 14, no. 1 (January 2003): 77–80. Accessed March 21, 2016. doi:10.1111/1467-9280.01422. http://pss.sagepub.com/content/14/1/77.short.

51) Marsh, Peter and Kate Fox. "Drinking and Public Disorder - Cross Cultural Comparisons." 1997. Accessed March 22, 2016. http://www.sirc.org/publik/ddbook6.html#_VPID_102.

52) Skogen, Jens Christoffer, Samuel B. Harvey, Max Henderson, Eystein Stordal, and Arnstein Mykletun. "Anxiety and Depression Among Abstainers and Low-Level Alcohol Consumers. The Nord-Trøndelag Health Study." *Addiction* 104, no. 9 (September 2009): 1519–29. doi:10.1111/j.1360-0443.2009.02659.x.

53) "Resources- Controlled Substance Schedules." Accessed March 22, 2016. http://www.deadiversion.usdoj.gov/schedules/.

54) "Busted - America's War on Marijuana." January 1998. Accessed March 23, 2016. http://www.pbs.org/wgbh/pages/frontline/shows/do pe/interviews/kleiman2.html.

55) Brown, Adam Tod. "How Fast Can You Get a Marijuana Prescription in California?" June 16, 2012. Accessed March 23, 2016. http://www.cracked.com/blog/how-fast-can-you-get-marijuana-prescription-in-california_p2/.

56) Network, Fusion Media. "Massive Millennial Poll." 2016. Accessed September 21, 2016. https://fusion.net/series/massive-millennial-poll/.

57) Blaszczak-Boxe, Agata. "Marijuana's History: How One Plant Spread Through the World." October 17, 2014. Accessed March 23, 2016.
http://www.livescience.com/48337-marijuana-history-how-cannabis-travelled-world.html.

58) Warf, Barney. "High Points: An Historical Geography of Cannabis." *Geographical Review* 104, no. 4 (September 25, 2014): 414–38. doi:10.1111/j.1931-0846.2014.12038.x.

59) Kepecs, Adam. *How Addictive Drugs Hijack Your Dopamine Systems*. September 13, 2010. Posted March 25, 2016. http://bigthink.com/videos/how-addictive-drugs-hijack-your-dopamine-systems.

Chapter 3 Takeaways:

- Pleasures like soda and TV are the caffeine of happiness, providing instant, short-lived boosts.
- We should *never* rely on pleasures to provide lasting happiness. Doing so leads to the Rock Star Lifestyle, addiction, and depression.
- Tempering our use of pleasures eases our hearts, minds, and wallets. The following strategies pave the way to a happier life:
  - Curate your social-media news feeds by unfollowing groups and people who don't interest you, and use social media as a way to facilitate meaningful connections, not waste time.
  - Eat fewer processed foods, and slow your eating pace to better gauge when your body is happily 80 percent full.
  - Replace mind-numbing video games with those that challenge your sense of creativity and strategy.
  - Enjoy the effects of narrative transport, but don't expect TV to ease stress like meditation or exercise.
  - Find your tipsy prime and set it as your default stopping point when drinking.
  - Enjoy safe, legal drugs, and avoid hard drugs at all costs. Don't let any drug replace your true happiness.
- With practice, our minds will begin preferring true happiness to instant gratification.

Coming Up in Chapter 4:

- Sleep and fitness: the essential foundations for a happy life
- How exercise is the miracle pill we're all looking for
  - How healthy people see the world differently
  - The epiphany inspiring a morbidly obese Millennial to lose 160 pounds
  - How to find exercise you'll actually *like*
- The *real* reason our bodies need sleep
  - A highly advanced, "new age" sleep schedule (which causes blackouts)
  - How to sleep without sacrificing your night life, according to science

Chapter 4
Sleep and Fitness: Building a Vehicle for Happiness

What man is happy? He who has a healthy body, a resourceful mind, and a docile nature.

—Thales

In college, my friend Claire was a notorious Debbie Downer. She'd find ways to be cynical in every scenario, from concerts to Ultimate Frisbee, and equally entertain and depress us with a sense of humor drier than a Martian desert. We affectionately dubbed her Eeyore, a nickname that she liked and actively tried to live up to. But one night, Eeyore crossed a line.

Given my love for positive psychology, people are often surprised to hear that my favorite music genre is heavy metal. I find the raw talent, vigor, and variety of instrumentation booming through my speakers. So anyways, back in college, as we spun records in the Vanderbilt radio station, I couldn't resist putting on some Black Sabbath. Naturally, Claire had been sassing everybody's music choices, but what she said next pushed me past my sass capacity.

"*This* is Black Sabbath? This guy can barely play guitar. My friend's band plays better than this."

She might as well have told the Pope her friend writes better books than the Bible. I was pretty ticked, but rather than counter her heresy with a lesson in metal history, I cut straight to the root of the problem.

"Eeyore, why do you have to be so . . . *Eeyore* all the time?"

"Because I haven't slept or exercised since high school."

Her instantaneous response surprised us. She didn't even have to think; she knew *exactly* what the problem was. The room sat in silence for a few more seconds as Ozzy continued wailing through the speakers.

Years later at a Vandy reunion, I caught up with Claire. She'd gone semi-pro in Ultimate Frisbee and had lost at least thirty pounds, and her career as a marine biologist was picking up steam. She carried a more vibrant and pleasant demeanor than I'd ever known from her. I commented on how she seemed less Eeyore-y, and asked what had changed.

"I just started taking care of myself, regular sleep schedule and running and whatnot, and everything else started falling into place!"

As we'll learn in this chapter, it really is that simple. We'll cover the surprising psychology linking fitness with our life goals, and delve into the hidden power of sleep. The purpose of this chapter is to begin building our bodies and minds into better vehicles for figuratively and literally navigating life, vehicles capable of hosting and nurturing the long-term happiness we'll collect throughout the rest of this book and in Volume II.

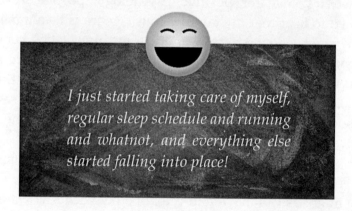

I just started taking care of myself, regular sleep schedule and running and whatnot, and everything else started falling into place!

Health and Fitness: My Only B in Eighth Grade

Every person, no matter how unfit he or she is, can rise a little higher, go a little faster, and grow to be a little stronger. The joy of surpassing the limits of the body is open to all.
— Mihaly Csikszentmihalyi

Laziness is a relatively new human luxury. Early on, only kings and politicians could afford to sit in chairs all day, and many of them died early because of it (if the arrows and poison didn't get 'em first). The rest of us normal folks had to till the fields and man the factories, and being sedentary meant the loss of a day's wages or fewer crops to reap.

In the modern era we can accomplish the day's tasks in as little as five hundred steps. The reduced need for physical labor across the first-world workforce has diminished the necessity and thus perceived benefits of physical fitness to function in modern society.

However, **our bodies are *begging* us to move around more, lest we become the lethargic human potatoes in *Wall-E.***

Exercise isn't just about getting a better Tinder picture. Hell, your beloved author works out or runs every single day, but I'm a naturally skinny guy (or as I prefer, *aerodynamic*). I'll probably never have bigger biceps than Michelle Obama, and that's fine; there are *far* more important reasons why I hit the gym.

Generation YMCA

Advertisements for CrossFit, Bowflex, and almost every gym out there love to show you how you'll *look* when you work out, but rarely, if ever describe how you'll *feel*, which is a much better value proposition. Having a better-looking body is just a small side effect of routine exercise; saying "work out because you'll look sexier" is like saying "buy a new car because it looks nicer." Both are accurate, but you buy a new car because it's more comfortable, efficient, powerful, and long lasting. We exercise because our minds and bodies experience a similar holistic upgrade.

According to the Harvard Fatigue Laboratory, which pioneered exercise research in the mid-twentieth century, consistent exercise has countless positive physiological effects on our bodies.[1] If I ran a gym, our ads would forgo touched-up images of washboard abs to list the following:

- Better sleep patterns
- Improved digestion
- Healthier immune system
- Increased brain activity, creativity, and memory
- More energy
- More confidence
- Reduced craving for unhealthy foods

Now, if you don't exercise regularly already, there's good news and bad news to digest before getting started (psychology tells us that delivering bad news first reduces worry, so here goes).[2] Some of us are preconditioned to view exercise as more difficult. Social scientist Emily Balcetis conducted a test where she had both "fit" and "unfit" people (defined by their waist-hip ratio) estimate the distance to a finish line across the room.[3] The unfit subjects saw the finish line as significantly farther than it really was, while fit folks found it closer. She concluded that our level of fitness actually changes how we view our environment and measure the difficulty of physical tasks. On a macro scale, mountains actually look smaller to your average fit person, while unfit people find them daunting, even insurmountable.

Let's look at the glass half full together; that *also* means that as we become more fit, we slowly begin to perceive physical tasks around us as easier. This segues us nicely into the good news. Remember the rate of diminishing returns we discussed in the pleasure chapter? Exercise provides the opposite effect, i.e., a rate of *increasing* returns. Once you overcome initial hurdles and can run, say, two miles without stopping, plenty of doors open to you. You can now more easily enjoy social exercise with others, such as doubles tennis or running a charity 5K, or enjoy a long afternoon hike without huffing and puffing, experiencing nature in a new way. Plus, you'll begin reaping the physiological effects listed above; you'll sleep better, feel better, have more focus, be smarter, more confident, and of course, look and feel more attractive.

It gets even better, because exercise rewards us neurologically as well. When you move yo' body, your brain recognizes this as a reaction to stress and engages fight-or-flight mode. The brain releases a chemical SWAT team known as brain-derived neurotrophic factor, or BDNF, which puts a hold on your regular neural activity and boosts adrenaline and endorphin levels. The flow of BDNF is why we feel pumped up yet clear-minded when we exercise. Plus, its release of endorphins has been likened to a narcotic high. Try visiting the finish line of a 10K race, and notice how everyone seems high as a kite, hugging, high-fiving, and sometimes even crying with bliss.

Liz, twenty-six, even used exercise to wean off of her addiction to pills entirely. "Endorphins are a more powerful drug than people realize," she says. She used to look forward to an evening alone with a pile of Vicodin. Now, "Any day where I meet with a cycling or speed-skating group I am crazy with excitement and anticipation!"

Getting Started

So clearly, exercise is a powerful avenue to long-term happiness. It provides countless physiological upgrades and catalyzes further happiness-building behavior, and as we'll discuss in the Chapter 6, helps us achieve an awesome feeling called "flow." But as I mentioned before, building exercise into your life from scratch is tough. So what advice do other Millennials have for us to help us become more active?

At 287 pounds, Norman was obese as a teen. Destined to underachieve at most sports, he felt he had few options for shedding pounds in high school. So he got creative. **Norman decided to try every activity out there until one stuck. "The most important** part of getting more active was finding that thing I loved to do," he says. He kicked off his fitness quest trying football, rugby, and wrestling, figuring his weight might prove some advantage. None of those held his interest, so he kept searching. What he eventually found surprised him. He had volunteered to create mixtapes for his suitemate's hip-hop dance crew, and one day figured *what the hell*, and joined them in a routine.

It wasn't love at first step, but he liked dance enough to keep coming back. "Once you find the activity that you really enjoy, you end up putting more time into it, and before you know it, you've dropped a few pounds," he says. For Norman, "a few" was fifty pounds lost on the dance floor. Today he looks trim and confident. "Take a hip-hop class, social dance, or Zumba dance class. Pick a routine and go for it!"

Norman's method of attack was variety; through trial and error, he found an activity that meant something to him and that he'd enjoy doing. Plus, he now has wicked hip-hop and ballroom dance skills.

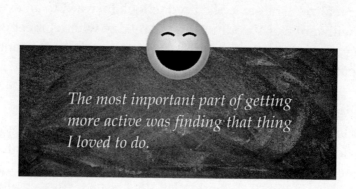

The most important part of getting more active was finding that thing I loved to do.

Norman's and Liz's stories show us that we may all have activities out there to discover and fall in love with. But what if we feel the cards are stacked against us from the start? What if we feel our bodies just weren't built for exercise?

Braden, twenty-nine, came from a heavier family and from childhood, felt he was genetically predisposed to be Santa Claus–shaped his entire life. For most of his twenties, he simmered in defeatist melancholy, settling into poor dietary choices and deteriorating health and happiness. Soon, he decided to reflect on his life and identify the culprits causing his plumpness. "Once I began changing habits like drinking too much soda, eating out often, and eating till I was full, it became much easier to lose weight," he says. "Once I stopped blaming bad genes or a slow metabolism, my attitude changed!" He asserts that once he overcame his initial mental and physical hurdles, going from flab to abs wasn't as hard as it seemed. "My motivation grew with every pound lost. It's difficult at times not to eat the whole pizza, but it's worth it."

Of everyone I spoke to, Daniel had the greatest mountain to climb. Remember him from the food section? Daniel weighed 360 pounds, or two Krispy Kremes away from needing a *Wall-E*-style hover chair. He recalls how on a high school band trip in Chicago, he had one too many bites of deep-dish pizza and the chair leg beneath him snapped. He went tumbling, speckling himself in pepperoni grease in front of all of his friends and classmates. "That should have been a wake-up call," he jokes.

Daniel had always dreamed he'd get fit to show everyone in his life he was capable of taking control. **Soon after the deep-dish disaster, he realized, "I can't keep a dream a dream forever. I saw it as two choices: live or die. Live by changing my life, or die before I got a chance to live it."**

In two years, he's lost 160 pounds. He likens the struggle of routine exercise to other life hurdles we've all overcome eventually. "Everyone at one point or another was scared to do something, like make new friends in grade school or enter the first serious relationships of their lives. Fight through it! Think about what the *future* will be like instead of dreading the present."

Our friends, family, and fellow Millennials are excellent sources of motivation to start and continue physical fitness. But what does *science* have to say about exercise motivation? Are there mind hacks that can get us (and keep us) going to the gym?

Eyes on the Prize

When they weren't teaching history or picking out inappropriately short shorts, our high school gym coaches loved to bellow, "Eyes on the prize! Eyes on the prize!" at us as we stationary-cycled our way to a B+. But do their obligatory words of encouragement hold weight in psychology?

Emily Balcetis furthered her experiments to find how we can motivate bodies and minds through the stresses of exercise. She tasked two groups with the same physical exercise; the baseline group was told to allow their minds to wander, while the second group was told to focus on the finish line as if it had a glowing halo around it. The focused group perceived the finish line 30 percent closer, moved 23 percent faster, and reported using 17 percent less exertion to reach their goal. **The adage "eyes on the prize," then, *does* hold weight in psychology, and we can use it to overcome the inertia of beginning an exercise habit.**

So how do we implement "eyes on the prize" in daily exercise? By picking a big goal, and using little goals to sling us there. "Narrowly focusing visual attention on a specific target, like a building a few blocks ahead, rather than looking around your surroundings, makes that distance appear shorter . . . and also makes exercising seem easier," says Dr. Balcetis.[4]

As mentioned above, exercise is literally addictive (in a good way). Eventually, our minds will begin to associate exercise with the euphoric surge of BDNF, and we'll continue training our bodies to routinely attain that feeling. To help us get to the point where exercise becomes autotelic, i.e., its own reward, psychologists say we can offer ourselves a more tangible reward. In his book *The Power of Habit*, Charles Duhigg recommends promising ourselves a bonus or a treat like a post-workout smoothie.[5] To get my own butt to the gym, I download new music from my favorite artists and tell myself I'm only allowed to listen to it at the gym.

The best compliment I ever received on my body was junior year in college when I donned a tank top and mesh shorts and sauntered outside to catch up with some friends playing Ultimate

Frisbee. **I passed a day-drunk fraternity guy who looked me up and down and went** *"Pshh,* **don't skip leg day, bro," which implies that I** *went to arm day.*

As I reflected on his "kind" words, I thought about how exercise had become a critical part of everyday happiness. My new and improved body allowed me to work longer and faster on Habitat for Humanity houses, hike the Grand Canyon base to rim in a single day, and accept a Vietnamese bodybuilder's push-up challenge (and lose gracefully). Outside of physical activity, my decent fitness level helps me sleep, drives me to eat healthy, and improves my focus and endurance in everyday activities. My personal health is as critical to my happiness as a DJ is to a dance party. Take it from Daniel, who's rocking a well-deserved Superman tank top: "Losing weight didn't just save me physically—it saved my happiness. Literally everything has gotten better!"

For some of us, reaching the point where exercise becomes autotelic, i.e., we just *want* to do it all the time, can be challenging. But by finding an activity enjoyable to you and keeping your eye on the prize, exercise will quickly become fun and expedite you to a happier life.

Now, heeding a passing sage's advice, I'm heading to the YMCA for leg day. Hopefully I'll exhaust myself enough to embrace another critical true happiness-building resource tonight.

Sleep: You Snooze, You Win

The way to a more productive, more inspired, more joyful life is getting enough sleep.
— Arianna Huffington

Ah sleep, you cruel mistress. You lure us to bed with promises of peace and tranquility only to disappear, leaving us tossing and turning in your absence. Why do you tease and torture us so? Eventually, we grow to resent you, avoiding you altogether. As you draw us to bed again, tears roll from our eyes as we push you away with caffeine or late-night Netflix. Eventually, we give in to your temptations, but the next morning you coldly depart, leaving us begging for your sweet return.

It's an unhealthy relationship for sure, but deep down, we know we can't live without you.

Sleeplessness isn't simply a problem exclusive to our generation, nor does it only plague industrialized societies as commonly believed. Researchers in Asia, Africa, Russia, Scandinavia, and even our own Centers for Disease Control in America agree: sleeplessness is a worldwide epidemic. Around 20 percent of adults in developing nations report insomnia or severe sleep disturbances, with even higher numbers across Western society.[6]

In America, we're among the worst at counting sheep. The CDC calls insufficient sleep a public-health crisis alongside smoking and HIV, with nearly 40 percent of Americans getting fewer than seven hours of sleep per night. An equal number of us report unintentionally nodding off in the middle of the day at least once a month. That's not planned naptime; that's falling asleep during meetings, dates, movies, and even behind the wheel.

So how do we Millennials stack up? Well, we're setting records again, but this one's not brag-worthy; **we're the most sleep-deprived generation in our nation's history**. We're a little worse than our parents, and *way* worse than our grandparents and their parents, who slept like rocks. In 1942, 84 percent of Americans reported getting the recommended seven to nine hours of sleep per night. Today, less than 30 percent of our generation reports getting enough sleep, meaning *most* of us might even qualify as clinical insomniacs, getting consistently six and a half or fewer hours of sleep per night.[7]

So what's keeping us awake that's more sleep-depriving than a *world war*?

Well, we're certainly not lacking any necessary ingredients. When we sleep, we sate a basic need like hunger or thirst, but unlike those other things, sleep doesn't require extrinsic resources. The Red Cross isn't airdropping Lunesta into refugee camps because our bodies naturally produce each chemical we need.

Rather, we're the victims of a vicious neurological cycle, swirling between stress, technology, and sleeplessness. Here's how it begins.

First, we feel stress. We process up to one hundred times more data per day than our great-grandparents' generation *and* work slightly longer hours, meaning we drown ourselves in cortisol, the stress-inducing chemical. If we haven't adequately processed our stress through exercise or meditation, it keeps us awake at night; it's harder for our brains to engage the sleep process if we're racked with worry.

Next, to numb our stresses or simply relax, we reach for a screen. Eighty-three percent of our generation sleeps next to our phones, and it's not a stretch to think our laptops and tablets are also close by. This behavior derails our mind's sleep-inducing process in two ways. First, seeing tweets, likes, and snaps releases stimulating dopamine, which forces the brain to shift gears and process new chemicals. Next, our LED-backlit screens emit blue-range light that disrupts our circadian rhythms by triggering the body into wakefulness and suppressing the production of melatonin, the sleep-inducing chemical. The dopamine and blue-light effect combine to create a "phase delay," during which our body thinks we're doing something important instead of sleeping, so it delays the sleep-inducing process for about thirty minutes.[8]

To summarize so far, as we're burning through season four of *Parks and Recreation* on our laptop at 12:18 a.m., we're giggling and relaxing, but inhibiting our sleep process. We're trading desperately needed shuteye for poorly timed pleasure.

The next day, our lack of sleep causes severe cognitive impairment. Our poor motor skills and sluggish reaction time affect our drive to work. When we get to the office or class, our lowered memory retention, prickly mood, and dulled social senses affect every task and interaction.

The net result of our lowered human performance is more stress, which despite our exhausted state, will keep us awake again tonight. And thus completes the cycle of modern sleeplessness: stress, technology, sleeplessness. Pretty soon we grow to resent the song we've chosen for our morning alarm ("All Along the Watchtower" triggers a nasty Pavlovian response from me now).

Here's why I think our generation's chronic sleeplessness is actually *good* news: it means we have *so much potential*. We're already the most eco-conscious, tolerant, altruistic, compassionate, and educated generation in our nation's history, and we accomplished all of this with *no sleep*. Just imagine what we can accomplish when we actually start sleeping and operating at our cognitive potentials!

So let's begin a snooze revolution.

Sleep Science: Why We Need it

In a competitive and individualistic society, it's easy to view sleep as an evolutionary impairment holding us back. After all, sleep takes time and time is money, so by the transitive property, sleep is a waste of money. If we think of our bodies as vehicles, a vehicle that shuts down every day for eight hours doesn't seem very efficient, does it? As Thomas Edison once put it, "Sleep is a criminal waste of time and a heritage to our cave days." Though can we really trust a sleep quote from a guy with stock in lightbulbs?

To circumvent the "problem" of sleep, mankind has been experimenting with stimulants and extreme sleep patterns for hundreds of years. During World War II, both Axis and Allied soldiers were issued amphetamines to combat fatigue.[9] Energy-drink consumption has increased five-fold since our generation began entering college in 1999. Some people have even tried a "polyphasic" sleep schedule, snoozing in short increments throughout the day. "Uberman" sleepers sleep just two and a half hours a day in evenly spaced twenty-minute naps. Their site asserts, "There is nothing known about the long-term side effects of being an Uberman," with the exception that sleepers on this schedule have been known to spontaneously black out.[10], [11]

What the Uber-goobers fail to appreciate is that sleep isn't a waste of time; it's waste management. As the cells in our body perform their daily functions, they produce waste, usually in the form of toxic proteins. To clear the waste, our body has a network of vessels called the lymphatic system, which picks up cell waste and dumps it into the bloodstream for disposal, a bit like a garbage man making his neighborhood rounds. The lymphatic system works 24/7 keeping our bodies clean.

Our brain, however, has no lymphatic vessels; the cells are just too densely packed and there's no space. So instead, the brain initiates a process neuroscientist Jeff Iliff calls "ingenious . . . and beautiful. An elegant design solution to some of the brain's most basic needs."[12] The brain stores cell waste for as long as necessary, then *flushes* itself clean using a chemical called cerebrospinal fluid, or CSF.

Here's why snoozing is important: our brain can only clean itself while in a sedative state we call sleep!

Good sleep, then, is like letting flight attendants clean out a plane between flights. The next day, when a new group of memories and thoughts boards, things move quickly and efficiently as they're supposed to. If we're getting inadequate sleep, we're forcing our new information to board a brain plane littered with garbage from the last flight. *God, it smells like feet in here! Is that a diaper in my seat?* If we don't let the CSF flight attendants do their job, we're allowing garbage to pile up between our cells. The next day, onboarding new information becomes a slow and unpleasant process.

Researchers have even begun linking sleep deprivation to severe mental illnesses. Over time, the buildup of cell waste protein amyloid-beta between our brain cells shuts down neural highways altogether, causing Alzheimer's.

So a thorough nightly brain shower is the best way to routinely maintain peak cognitive ability. This philosophy is gospel to NASA, which, regardless of the mission severity, *always* schedules its astronauts to get at least eight hours of sleep.[13] Considering it costs $350,000 per *hour* to run the International Space Station, it's safe to say Houston has weighed the cost-to-benefit ratio in favor of sweet shuteye.[14]

It's no surprise, then, that some of the most successful Millennials out there adhere to strict sleeping schedules to stay sharp, as well. Jordan Fliegel, founder of CoachUp, considers sleep part of his work schedule. He wants us to remember that "you're being counterproductive by avoiding either fitness or sleep in exchange for extra hours of banging on your keyboard." To destress before bed, he meditates for ten minutes. Emily Rasowsky, founder of the Women in Tech campaign, unplugs from her phone and computer at least thirty minutes before bed. "Keeping the lights dim for the last hour helps a lot!"[15]

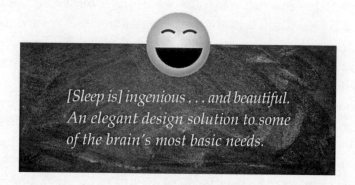

[Sleep is] ingenious . . . and beautiful.
An elegant design solution to some
of the brain's most basic needs.

Besides lowering our stress levels and dimming the lights, what else can we do to shake hands with Mr. Sandman?

First, cool down the bedroom. The National Institute of Health found that a cool head and a warm body maximizes metabolic rate and the flow of CSF. Dutch researchers pinpointed the ideal sleeping temperature to be 63–65 degrees Fahrenheit, but this may vary if you grew up in Canada or Miami. The overall point is to make your bedroom a little too cool for you to sit in, but perfectly cozy under the comforters.[16]

As for the ideal sleeping position, scientists can't decide whether on your back or side is best. Both positions relax your spine and optimize breathing, though a 2015 study published in *The Journal of Neuroscience* indicates that sleeping on your side may boost the flow of CSF.[17] Plus, sleeping on your side opens you up to be big/little spoon.

Really, though, there's not enough definitive research behind either position to recommend one over the other—it comes down to your personal preference. Just be sure in either position you're using just one pillow; this best aligns your spine and neck and opens your trachea for better sleep quality and less snoring.

Whatever you do, though, *don't* fall asleep on your chest. I used to do this in college if I'd had a few too many beers before coming home. I called it the "sloppy spread eagle." **Aside from being in the ignominious and embarrassing "passed out" position, sleeping on our face compresses our chest, restricts breathing, and strains our neck muscles. It's a chiropractor's nightmare . . . or best friend, since face sleepers feed her business.**

If you tend to roll onto your chest during the night, try reducing the ambient light in your room so you're less likely to subconsciously roll away from it, and tightening your covers to restrict your movements.

SIDE

Pros: CSF flow, spooning.

Cons: accelerated aging, numb arms.

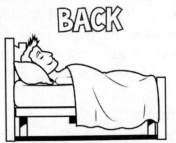

BACK

Pros: spine alignment, blood flow.

Cons: snoring.

"SLOPPY SPREAD EAGLE"

Pros: friends may predict hangover and make breakfast.

Cons: poor breathing, abysmal sleep quality.

How about wake-up routines? How can we catapult out of bed with a smile to rise, shine, and conquer? Caffeine isn't the only stimulant at our disposal in the morning. Vitamin D from sunlight signals our internal clocks to shift into wakefulness mode, and we can begin accumulating it while we sleep by leaving our blinds open and allowing the sun to ease us awake. Once we're out of bed, just fifteen seconds of exercise will send endorphins rushing through our body, like turning the key in our ignition. I like to do jumping jacks and push-ups in the morning; my friend Matt does shadowboxing, while my friend Jenny performs tai chi.

All right, so we've talked about the importance of sleep and reviewed a few tips for getting in and out of our body's sleep mode. Let's say you've begun adequately destressing before bed through exercise or meditation (addressed in the next chapter), and are beginning to fall asleep at a reasonable hour in your cooled-down, single-pillow sleep haven. You've engaged a blissful rhythm during the workweek where you're asleep by elevenish and up by seven, no longer an insomnia statistic. The days where you wake up with a string of profanity and a blind slap of the snooze button are becoming fewer and fewer, and instead you're waking up to freshly washed, high-speed neural highways. Your early-morning feelings of empowerment, energy, and joy begin to last all day.

Then the weekend rolls around. Suddenly, your plans *start* at your usual bedtime. As your friends text you the logistics for barhopping, you fight off unwelcome yawns. Maybe you have Kanye tickets, but he won't be on until midnight—and you know if he catches you falling asleep at his show, he'll have you *killed*.

You don't want to miss the weekend's late-night shenanigans, but also don't want to disobey your body's signals. What now?

Circadian Rhythms and Social Jet Lag

When our sleep schedules misalign with our social plans, we're forced to make a tough choice. Do we cave in to our body's signals and sacrifice some fun? Or do we brew some coffee and later face the consequences of pushing our minds into overdrive?

Scientists call this quandary "social jet lag" and have concluded that powering through our tiredness to party is fine, as long as we wake up within an hour of the usual time the next morning. *What? You mean when we stumble home from the post-postgame, we should set our alarms for 9 a.m.? Our roommates are going to smack us like a human snooze button!*

Here's why sleeping in on weekends is a bad call. If we suddenly go to sleep later *and* wake up later, we throw off our circadian rhythm, or our body's internal clock, hence the term "social jet lag." Throwing off our clocks not only keeps us up later Sunday night when we're trying to snooze before work, but causes hormonal imbalance and releases ghrelin into our brains, causing unnecessary hunger. This is why researchers often link poor sleep habits to diabetes and obesity.[18]

We can avoid the nastiness associated with social jet lag by either going to sleep or waking up at the same time as we have been during the week. If we can wake up around the usual time on Saturday and Sunday, we're telling our bodies, "Last night was a one-time thing." In general, our minds receive this message much better than the person in bed next to us.

All right, so it's 9 a.m. on a Saturday and we're doing jumping jacks/tai chi to wake up, but we've got a *long* day ahead of us. We've got brunch and mimosas whenever our friends arise, Ultimate Frisbee at four, and another party at 11:30 tonight. No way we're going to make it. How do we run this social marathon without enough sleep from the night before?

Your Snooze Toolkit: Nappucinos and Siestas

> *Learn from yesterday, live for today, look to tomorrow, rest this afternoon.*
>
> —Charles Schultz,
> *Charlie Brown's Little Book of Wisdom*

What do Napoleon, Churchill, Einstein, and dozens of US presidents all have in common? That's right, they all conquered guys with terrible moustaches. Also, they were nappers.

Historically, we've had an odd stigma against napping in America. We often think of it as a time-waster or a retreat for the young or sickly. We scarcely hear calls for "naptime!" after our preschool years. In a work environment, someone caught catching z's at their desk is subject to judgment or even punishment.

Yet, all around the world and throughout history, people have had naps built into their daily schedule to reenergize before catapulting into the rest of the day. Portugal, Spain, the Philippines, and much of Latin America practice the *siesta* after lunch. Countries in North Africa and the Middle East practice similar midday respite, in part to avoid the hottest part of the day. **Even Japan and China, countries known for a brutal, sometimes inhumane work culture, strongly believe in midday naps.**

In China, naps are written into the Constitution. While working in Beijing, my friend Spencer was able to indulge this delightful right, napping up to an hour during the workday. "Believe me, I took advantage of it along with everyone else."

So are these other countries gaining something from midday snoozes, or are siestas just an unnecessary foreign tradition to skip, like goulash or fire walking?

To begin addressing that question, let's go back to our circadian rhythms. You may find that despite your passionate adherence to the 80 percent eating rule, you still feel a bit sluggish after lunch. Don't blame your Chipotle burrito bowl; it's your biological clock knocking you out. A 1986 study by the Institute of Circadian Physiology found that subjects with a full night's sleep in a time-free environment (where they couldn't judge the time of day) consistently felt the urge to sleep in the afternoon. A further thirty years of research into the subject has led researchers to a surprising consensus: a midafternoon snooze is actually a part of our circadian rhythms, one that we've misguidedly suppressed in Western work culture.[19]

Why does our brain want to nap in the afternoon? From the moment we're awake, our brains begin building up homeostatic drive, a.k.a. the urge to sleep again. To keep us awake, the brain buffers this bedtime prep work by simultaneously producing an alerting signal, essentially building a dam to hold back our growing sleepiness. Then at bedtime, the alerting signal fizzles out, unleashing the day's buildup to lull us into sleep. However, researchers have discovered a dip in the power of the alerting signal right in the middle of our waking hours, usually after lunch, a time Harvard researcher Charles Czeisler calls "a great time for a nap."[20]

Okay, that explains *what's* going on, but *why* does the alertness signal dip when it could keep us powered on throughout the day? Sleep scientists are still investigating, but it's likely because our brains value the power of a good nap.

So what *is* the power of a good nap?

Well, there are two types of naps we can take with different effects: the popular Western "power nap" or the full, 90- to 120-minute siesta. Let's talk power naps first.

Social psychologist James Maas coined the term "power nap" in 1998 to describe a nap long enough to gain some cognitive benefits, but short enough to fit into a normal workday. Australian researchers, having studied various naptimes up to thirty minutes, determined that the ten-minute power nap is best, greatly reducing fatigue and boosting our cognitive performance for the rest of the day.[21]

Now you may think, *Why waste time on naps when we have caffeine?* But why not have two awesome things at once? British researchers found that since caffeine takes up to thirty minutes to affect our brains, downing a coffee just before a power nap springloads our minds so we experience a double shot of energy when we wake up.[22] Some researchers call this a *stimulant nap,* or more colloquially, a *nappuccino.* Ellie, a twenty-six-year-old pediatric emergency-room nurse, takes nappucinos during every shift. "I couldn't live without them—they help me launch into the weird hours of my job!"

All right, let's summarize thus far: after our ten-minute investment, a power nap will suppress our fatigue, boost our performance, double our alertness, improve our mood, and according to the Chinese government, greatly increase our production of iPhones and Nike shoes. Sounds like a holistic winner. So why do other countries bother going down for siestas that can last up to two and a half hours? The answer lies within the deepest stages of our sleep.

As I touched on earlier, power naps *avoid* deep sleep; this way they're short and practical, but won't reap the whopping benefits of reaching our body's mysterious final stage of sleep: rapid eye movement, or REM. Characterized by the twitching of our eyes within our eyelids, REM sleep is when our brains operate at an extremely high level, processing and storing the day's information, cleaning themselves, and maintaining neural connections.

REM sleep is also when our dreams occur, though scientists aren't entirely sure why we dream at all. Francis Crick, co-discoverer of DNA, believes our dreams are the result of randomly activated neural connections as the brain performs maintenance on itself. **French neurophysiologist Michel Jouvet believes the brain flashes images during dreams to solicit and rehearse certain emotions.**[23] **What emotions my brain is trying to rehearse while I'm riding dinosaurs with Hillary Clinton is beyond me.**

To keep us from kicking our spooning partners in real life, our brains also shut off all of our voluntary muscles during REM sleep, an effect called "sleep paralysis." The reason why we're often unable to scream or run away in our dreams is because we're genuinely paralyzed in real life.

It takes a full ninety minutes for the brain to work up to REM sleep, but the process only lasts a few minutes. So why do our dreams seem to last hours, even days? Remember, our brains are operating at light speed; we can dream hours worth of material in just a few minutes, and once the brain completes a two-hour cycle in and out of REM sleep, it usually doesn't store the memories of the dreams. We only remember our dreams when we're interrupted during REM before our brains can dispose of the erroneous memories.

If we sleep a full eight hours, we're getting a solid four REM cycles in. Here's where the siesta comes in; adding an extra REM cycle to our daily routine allows our mind to finish maintenance from the night before or begin cataloguing and storing what we've already processed before lunch. The tangible advantages of investing in a full siesta over a power nap is improved energy, creativity, and memory.

So what are some real-world examples of when we should leverage power naps over siestas, and vice versa? If you're a fast-moving, frappe-chugging consultant with an impending deadline, consider a *nappuccino* to regain your focus and stay near your cognitive peak without losing much time. If you've been studying all day before an evening exam, or have a big game coming up, consider a full siesta to allow your mind time to catalogue and organize and your body to refill your energy wells.

Life Is a Highway

When I'm not writing about happiness I also love to write about cars. I write for a few medium-sized publications and sites, and a huge perk of my hobby is that I'll often get a shiny new model for a whole week to cruise around in and write about. I've had everything from bare-bones $17K Jeeps to fully loaded $100K Mercedes, three Teslas to the woeful Mitsubishi Mirage. During my automotive odysseys, I've found that people generally underestimate the value of a nice car until they get in one for long enough. Nice cars aren't just faster; they make you feel more safe, confident, in control, and capable. Even as a sitting duck in rush-hour traffic, you feel holistically better in a Mercedes than a Dodge.

Having a healthy body and mind feels the same way. After a few weeks of adequate sleep and exercise, as your body transforms from an old Toyota into a Lexus, every second of your life becomes more comfortable and enjoyable. But unlike a new Lexus, a new body and mind don't cost $80,000—just some time, discipline, and effort.

Start building your happiness Lexus right away by exercising today and sleeping better tonight. If you don't already have a preferred method of exercise, sign up for a variety of classes and find one. The sooner your exercise regimen becomes autotelic, the faster you'll build your Lexus. When going gets tough, keep your eyes on the prize and find little micro-goals to work toward, like reaching the next block or performing three more reps.

Tonight, create your sleep haven by cooling your room, minimizing late-night laptop work, and sleeping on your side or back. In the morning, turn your ignition with some sunlight and light exercise. With these simple lifestyle changes, you'll soon sense that you're piloting a better vehicle for building happiness.

But sleep and fitness aren't the only ways to optimize your body for true happiness. A third practice exists, one that's quickly becoming a mainstay in the daily regimen of the world's happiest and most successful people.

References:

1) Tipton, C. M. "Contemporary Exercise Physiology: Fifty Years After the Closure of Harvard Fatigue Laboratory." *Exercise and sport sciences reviews*. 26 (August 11, 1998): 315–39. Accessed April 3, 2016. http://www.ncbi.nlm.nih.gov/pubmed/9696994.

2) Legg, Angela M. and Kate Sweeny. "Do You Want the Good News or the Bad News First? The Nature and Consequences of News Order Preferences." *Personal Social Psychological Bulletin*. October 31, 2013. Accessed April 3, 2016. doi:10.1177/0146167213509113. http://psp.sagepub.com/content/early/2013/10/30/014 6167213509113.abstract.

3) Balcetis, Emily. *Why Some People Find Exercise Harder Than Others*. November 25, 2014. Posted April 5, 2016. https://www.ted.com/talks/emily_balcetis_why_some_p eople_find_exercise_harder_than_others?language=en.

4) "Keeping Your Eyes on the Prize Can Help with Exercise, Psychology Study Finds." October 1, 2014. Accessed April 5, 2016. http://www.nyu.edu/about/news-publications/news/2014/october/keeping-your-eyes-on-the-prize-can-help-with-exercise.html.

5) Duhigg, Charles. *The Power of Habit: Why We Do What We Do in Life and Business*. New York: Random House Publishing Group, 2012.

6) Stranges, S., W. Tigbe, F. X. Gómez-Olivé, M. Thorogood, and N. B. Kandala. "Sleep Problems: An Emerging Global Epidemic? Findings from the INDEPTH WHO-SAGE Study Among More Than 40,000 Older Adults from 8 Countries Across Africa and Asia." *Sleep*. 35,

no. 8 (August 2, 2012): 1173–81. Accessed April 21, 2016.
http://www.ncbi.nlm.nih.gov/pubmed/22851813.

7) Jones, Jeffrey M. "In U.S., 40% Get Less Than Recommended Amount of Sleep." December 19, 2013. Accessed April 13, 2016.
http://www.gallup.com/poll/166553/less-recommended-amount-sleep.aspx.

8) Cajochen, Christian, Sylvia Frey, Doreen Anders, Jakub Späti, Matthias Bues, Achim Pross, Ralph Mager, Anna Wirz-Justice, and Oliver Stefani. "Evening Exposure to a Light-Emitting Diodes (LED)-Backlit Computer Screen Affects Circadian Physiology and Cognitive Performance." *Journal of Applied Physiology* 110, no. 5 (May 1, 2011): 1432–38. Accessed April 12, 2016.
doi:10.1152/japplphysiol.00165.2011.
http://jap.physiology.org/content/110/5/1432.full.pdf+html.

9) "A Brief History of Methamphetamine - Alcohol and Drug Abuse Information - Vermont Department of Health." 2016. Accessed April 21, 2016.
http://healthvermont.gov/adap/meth/brief_history.aspx.

10) "Uberman Sleep." July 29, 2012. Accessed April 21, 2016.
https://www.polyphasicsociety.com/polyphasic-sleep/overviews/uberman-2/.

11) Isaacson, Betsy. "Our Sleep Problem and What to Do about It." *Newsweek* (Newsweek Europe). January 22, 2015.
http://www.newsweek.com/2015/01/30/our-sleep-problem-and-what-do-about-it-301165.html.

12) Iliff, Jeff. *One More Reason to Get a Good Night's Sleep.* October 13, 2014. Posted April 21, 2016.
https://www.ted.com/talks/jeff_iliff_one_more_reason_to_get_a_good_night_s_sleep?language=en.

13) May, Sandray. "Sleeping in Space." June 8, 2015. Accessed April 21, 2016.
http://www.nasa.gov/audience/foreducators/stem-on-station/ditl_sleeping.

14) Fishman, Charles. "5,200 Days in Space." *The Atlantic* (The Atlantic), August 20, 2015. http://www.theatlantic.com/magazine/archive/2015/01/5200-days-in-space/383510/.

15) *The Sleep Habits of These Successful Millennials Could Change the Way You Work. The Huffington Post.* January 5, 2016. http://www.huffingtonpost.com/2016/01/04/sleep-habits-of-successful-Millennials_n_8838114.html.

16) Heid, Markham. "Is Sleeping in a Cold Room Better for You?" November 26, 2014. Accessed April 21, 2016. http://time.com/3602415/sleep-problems-room-temperature/.

17) Lee, Hedok, Lulu Xie, Mei Yu, Hongyi Kang, Tian Feng, Rashid Deane, Jean Logan, Maiken Nedergaard, and Helene Benveniste. "The Effect of Body Posture on Brain Glymphatic Transport." *The Journal of Neuroscience* 35, no. 31 (August 5, 2015): 11034–44. Accessed September 21, 2016. doi:10.1523/JNEUROSCI.1625-15.2015. http://www.jneurosci.org/content/35/31/11034.short.

18) Wong, Patricia M., Brant P. Hasler, Thomas W. Kamarck, Matthew F. Muldoon, and Stephen B. Manuck. "Social Jetlag, Chronotype, and Cardiometabolic Risk." *The Journal of Clinical Endocrinology & Metabolism* 100, no. 12 (November 18, 2015): 4612–20. doi:10.1210/jc.2015-2923.

19) Goleman, Daniel. "Feeling Sleepy? An Urge to Nap Is Built in." *The New York Times.* September 12, 1989. http://www.nytimes.com/1989/09/12/science/feeling-sleepy-an-urge-to-nap-is-built-in.html?pagewanted=all.

20) Lambert, Craig. "Deep into Sleep." July 1, 2005. Accessed April 21, 2016. http://harvardmagazine.com/2005/07/deep-into-sleep.html.

21) Brooks, A. and L. Lack. "A Brief Afternoon Nap Following Nocturnal Sleep Restriction: Which Nap Duration Is Most Recuperative?" *Sleep*. 29, no. 6 (June 27, 2006): 831–40. Accessed April 21, 2016. https://www.ncbi.nlm.nih.gov/pubmed/16796222.

22) Reyner, L. A. and J. A. Horne. "Suppression of Sleepiness in Drivers: Combination of Caffeine with a Short Nap." *Psychophysiology* 34, no. 6 (December 24, 1997): 721–25. Accessed April 21, 2016. http://www.ncbi.nlm.nih.gov/pubmed/9401427.

23) Purves, D., G. L. Augustine, D. Fitzpatrick, and et al. *The Possible Functions of REM Sleep and Dreaming*. 2nd ed. MA: Sinauer Associates, 2001. http://www.ncbi.nlm.nih.gov/books/NBK11121/.

Chapter 4 Takeaways:

- Adequate sleep and exercise are essential to living life longer and fuller.
- Exercise provides a holistic upgrade to our bodies and minds. Even minor efforts to exercise will boost our energy levels, immune systems, and brain functions.
  - To quickly fall in love with exercise, explore a variety of activities until one sticks.
  - Sling yourself to higher physical achievement by keeping your eyes on the prize and routinely chasing smaller goals.
- Sleep is the brain's way of cleaning itself and maintaining optimal cognition each day.
  - Turn your bedroom into a "sleep haven" by cooling down your room, using one pillow, and resisting electronics in bed.
  - Try a ten-minute nappuccino for a quick cognitive boost, and a full siesta to kill tiredness and conquer the rest of the day.

Coming Up in Chapter 5:

- Meditation, and why Oprah and Google employees bother with this quirky, 2,500-year-old exercise
- How eight days in a Buddhist monastery permanently changed my brain
- Harvard and Yale scientists stumble upon the hidden benefits of meditation
- A six-foot-three human tree tries yoga (and five other meditation techniques)

Chapter 5
Meditation: Building a Better Brain

Everything is so bright, so crisp . . . this is not the synthetic, always-just-about-to-end buzz of drugs. This is roughly a thousand times better. It's the best high of my life.
—Dan Harris on meditation, *10% Happier*

When most of us think *meditation*, we picture monks on a misty mountaintop humming *ohm* in harmony, punctuated by the occasional strike of the gong. Or, we may think of that guy with the man bun in our dorm sitting cross-legged before a bundle of cindering incense.

In today's progressive America, a more clean-shaven population is taking meditation more seriously. Many Fortune 500 companies are adopting meditation practices if they haven't already, including Google, General Mills, Target, and Proctor & Gamble. Government entities such as prisons, schools, and even the Marine Corps have begun advocating cross-legged quiet time, along with some of the greatest athletes of our time: Kobe Bryant, LeBron James, Derek Jeter, and our Olympic gold-medalist volleyball duo Misty May-Treanor and Kerry Walsh.

So what exactly is meditation, and what is everyone trying to get out of it? Does it really work, or in the words of Alec Baldwin's character on *30 Rock*, is it "a waste of time, like learning French or kissing after sex"? In this chapter, we'll hear a tale of how meditation cleansed the grimy mind of one Millennial (hello!), talk with some other Millennials who've enhanced their lives through meditation, and recap the cold science for why it works, including a recent discovery that blew the hats off of Harvard researchers and the scientific community as a whole. Finally, we'll wrap up by leading you into your first week of meditation, so you can begin experiencing the benefits to body and mind.

So get ready for a mental cleanse.

Eight Days in Buddhist Boot Camp

"I'm really stuck with meditation. I'm just not getting anywhere with it," I told Hill, my bohemian stepcousin I introduced in the True Happiness chapter. We were sipping smoothies under a cool, midwinter Atlanta sun, catching some desperately needed Vitamin D.

Despite his daily ragtag appearance, Hill is highly intelligent and recklessly adventurous, like Indiana Jones but with a love for puppets and unicorn pajamas over aboriginal treasures. Hill and I share a love for wild, new experiences and being yes-men, but while I had gone corporate after college, he went off the grid to quest across the country like an eccentric, bandana-wearing Odysseus.

So when I learned he had spent six months in a Buddhist monastery, I was hardly surprised. In fact, his time there had inspired him to write his own book on happiness (*Blue: A Mindfulness Tale*). Turns out, the monks operate the monastery like an AirBnB, so just about anyone can come live, eat, play, and meditate with them. Room and board was just forty dollars a night, so I was sold.

In the weeks leading up to my stay in the monastery, I played a game called *Lumosity* on my iPhone. The game trains and scores various aspects of your cognitive functioning such as your speed, memory, attention, and problem solving. I used the game to create a benchmark for my pre-meditation brain. That way, after meditating for a while, I could objectively quantify meditation's effects on my brain. Before I left for the monastery, I'd peaked at a score of 1,311.

So on a chilly, overcast Friday afternoon, I packed my car, solemnly ate my last non-vegan meal for the week, and set off for my monastic adventure.

Magnolia Grove Monastery was started by Thich Nhat Hanh, the spiritual leader of modern Vietnamese Buddhism. Found deep in the bracken woods of Northern Mississippi, the monastery is home to twenty-five devout Buddhist brothers and sisters who have devoted their lives to studying and sharing the messages of Buddhism, mindfulness, and meditation.

I had tried meditating before but these were the big leagues. There was no "meditation for noobs" course here, and the purity and sanctity of the monastic practices attracted veteran yogis (meditators) from around the country. I was among Jedi Masters and Jedi Knights, yet with my current skills I couldn't Force push a pencil off a table.

It became immediately clear that I wouldn't be pampered as a Padawan either. I arrived shortly before 9 p.m., allowing a young monk just enough time to show me the grounds, the schedule, and my bed before he suddenly stopped answering my questions, returning my inquiries with a polite smile, nod, and finger over his lips. Turns out, Noble Silence was from 9 p.m. to 9 a.m. My next objective was to attend my first sitting meditation at 5:30 a.m.

After a few hours of sleep, I showered and followed a fellow yogi through the icy grass to the grand meditation hall, a surprisingly modern-looking building with a vibrant red roof and a gray-brick exterior. Men entered from the right, where both yogis and monks slipped off our frosty shoes and shuffled into the great hall. The women appeared from the left. Due to Noble Silence lasting another four hours, eye contact was followed by more smiles and nods, otherwise there was an oddly calming lack of communication.

In stark contrast to the Catholic chapels I dozed off in growing up, the Buddhist meditation hall was elegantly simple: no columns, pews, or stained-glass windows depicting angels smiting Satan. The only pieces of furniture to speak of were fifty or so square, chocolate-brown mats topped with puffy round pillows, divided to keep the genders separated and positioned to face the windows. The center of the hall held an elegant bouquet of unrecognizable flora and a cauldron-like drum manned by a tiny, androgynous monk. Only the sound of socks shuffling on the hardwood floor punctuated the silence.

I popped a squat at a meditation station next to an older monk, squirming to find a position I could commit to for an undefined amount of time. Legs crossed, butt-to-pillow seemed to be a winner.

I'd read Thich Nhat Hanh's book *Happiness* prior to the experience so I knew the basics: sit still, breath slow, clear my mind. I'd memorized one of his breathing poems to help get me through my first meditation lasting more than five minutes:

> *In. Out.*
> *Deep. Slow.*
> *Calm. Ease.*
> *Smile. Release.*
> *Present Moment. Wonderful Moment.*

With three strikes of the gong-like drum, my first foray into true meditation began.

To explain the purpose of meditation, and to understand why fifteen minutes later I almost went bat-s*** insane, let's go back 2,500 years to the origins of Buddhism: a tale of a wayward twentysomething many of us may identify with.

Buddhism Basics

Buddha, born Siddhartha, was the son of a Nepalese king who was prophesied to grow up to either become a great spiritual leader or a great king. His father, vying for the latter, began stacking the cards in his favor. He kept Sid confined within the palace walls so he wouldn't discover suffering and would become accustomed to a life of luxury he'd never want to give up. Eager to understand the world, Sid begged his father for decades to allow him to venture beyond walls, so eventually his father gave in. Sort of.

The king ensured all signs of suffering—the old, the sick, the poor—were removed from sight, and allowed his son only to stay within walking distance of the palace. Catching on to the ploy, Sid stole a horse and rode beyond the limits of his father's Hollywood set. On his very first quest outside of his one-percenter bubble, Sid discovered age, sickness, death, and poverty, and grew compassion for his fellow man. After contemplating the fragility of existence, Siddhartha shed his earthly belongings and began a spiritual journey across Nepal and India. His objective? To understand and potentially conquer suffering.

Now in his late twenties, Sid tried some mainstay spiritual practices of the day, from holding his breath underwater to self-flagellation. After living on one grain of rice a day and nearly starving, he concluded that abusing the physical self wasn't the way to the enlightenment he sought. He had five followers for a while, but once they discovered his lavish past, they abandoned him, figuring enlightenment would never come to a trust-fund baby. After years of failing to find answers, a thirty-five-year-old Siddhartha sat below a tree on the outskirts of Bodhi, India, and vowed not to stand until he had conquered his subconscious and achieved enlightenment.

Siddhartha began meditating below the tree, but instead of worshipping a deity or repenting his sins, he just . . . *chilled out.* He counted his breaths, enjoyed the sunlight, and listened to the ants scurry beneath him. As time passed, his stress evaporated; he felt sublime relaxation, and his mental clock stopped counting the minutes.

Eventually, Sid reached a deep, trance-like state where he came face to face with Mara, the demon lord of ego and illusion. Mara first fired a volley of flaming arrows at Siddhartha, but Sid calmly turned them to lotus blossoms. Mara then tried to torment and manipulate Siddhartha by seducing him with his demon daughters, but Sid figuratively swiped left; he neither averted his gaze nor willed Mara or his daughters away—he simply looked upon them indifferently.

With his mind no longer twisted nor tormented by Mara's tricks, Siddhartha realized that Mara was simply a projection of his own subconscious, and learned that he and Mara were one.

Following this revelation, Siddhartha became the first Buddha, or Enlightened One.

His teachings on enlightenment spawned a new religion, though many consider Buddhism to be a philosophy and even a psychotherapy. Buddha himself is more of a professor than a deity; he's the world's oldest self-help guru, aiding billions in achieving happiness through self-awareness and enlightenment. Buddhist monks devote their entire lives to pursuing and understanding enlightenment so they may perpetuate Buddha's teachings and help all who are interested grow to love and understand their subconscious.

At War with Silence

Sadly, fifteen minutes into my own meditation, my subconscious and I were at each other's throats. I was battling my own Mara and losing. Thich Nhat Hanh tells us, "Don't just do something, sit there," but I found this immensely more anguishing than he led on. **While I had been numbing my mind for years with beer, Netflix, and loud music, negative and pointless thoughts and memories had amassed, pounding and slobbering on the walls of my subconscious like Wal-Mart shoppers on Black Friday.** When I finally closed my eyes with no distractions or numbing agents present, I let those negative emotions and random thoughts come tumbling in.

Will I ever finish this book? Man, I really blew it with Anna at formal five years ago . . . let's replay that whole night. I wonder if my third-grade teacher hated me. Why haven't they made a Matrix prequel?

My mind was racing like a badly behaved child before bedtime. My thoughts violently swarmed like the furious former residents of a disrupted beehive. To slow them, I refocused on my breathing. *In . . . Out . . . Deep . . . Calm . . .*

Thirty minutes into meditation my eyelids stopped twitching and my breathing slowed, but the string of random, often negative thoughts continued.

Robert Downey Jr. is overrated—he just has good facial hair and never smiles. Now remembering a few times I got yelled at as a child . . .

I wonder what Ralph Nader is doing right now. Why do I keep going to Taco Bell?

Again, I returned to my breathing exercise. *In . . . Out . . . Deep . . . Calm . . .* Soon, the swarm dispersed and the velocity of my thoughts lowered. I started noticing the white noise in the room, then the gentle breathing of the monk beside me. My upper back ached from sustained pseudo-lotus pose, but per Thich Nhat Hanh's advice, I "noted" the discomfort and put it out of focus.

Then something amazing happened.

Suddenly, I felt my mind was hundreds of feet above my body, past the clouds of the winter storm and settling into the tranquil, teal sky above. I sensed a presence before me—a face inches from mine above the clouds. The presence was a welcome one, like a cross between an old friend and a doppelganger (it's worth pointing out at this point that I'm awake and sober).

So about thirty-five minutes into my first hardcore meditation exercise, I felt out-of-body relaxation, a neurologically explicable phenomenon we'll get to later. I carried this feeling for the next twenty-five minutes until a soft gong signified the end of morning meditation.

It wasn't an easy journey; my subconscious had pelted me with pointless thoughts and repressed memories such as failed romances, my first car crash, and pop culture garbage. However, by returning to my breathing and reciting the breathing poem, I was able to navigate the storm and end in calm waters.

The takeaway so far, of course, isn't to sit and meditate for an hour until you feel good. I took a prolonged "dose" of meditation to better understand its effects and accelerate my learning, but the monks and I don't recommend you do this. Instead, we've codeveloped a beginner's meditation schedule that we'll take a look at later. For now, back to the monastery.

The monks and I meditated up to two hours per day, in sessions ranging from ten minutes to an hour. Each time I closed my eyes and faced my subconscious, it smeared more sewage into my frame of focus: one of my rare fights with my sister, failed jokes, the annoyingly catchy "Mmmbop" by Hansen. But each time, I was better able to place these thoughts aside, forgive myself for past transgressions, and refocus on my breathing. Meditation was becoming easier. Plus, after just a few collective hours, I was able to *feel* the benefits. My resting heart rate slightly dropped, my information retention increased, and for the first time in a decade, I could lie awake at night unafraid of my own mental chatter and without the craving to numb myself with TV or music. As a result, my dreams have become more blissful, vivid, and memorable.

My lifelong war with my subconscious was coming to a truce, raising my hedonic set point and paving the way to a happier and more efficient lifestyle of mindfulness: an amazing voluntary mindset that we'll cover in Chapter 6. I sincerely hadn't expected to be this smitten with meditation.

Now, a naysayer may say, "Nay . . . living in a monastery and claiming your mind felt relaxed is like living in a spa and claiming your body felt relaxed. No duh!" So will meditation integrate well into the hustle and bustle of real life? Do we all have to eat vegan for a week and meditate for hours surrounded by monks and gongs to reap the benefits?

Beyond the Monastery

To find out, I enlisted my first guinea pigs upon leaving the monastery—my seventeen-year-old cousin, Henry, and my Uncle Dave, a high-powered corporate lawyer. Growing up as one of four boys, my Uncle Dave wasn't one to sugarcoat feedback. Family gatherings were a verbal boxing match between the four brothers, who threw hilarious but honest jabs at each other's livelihoods, professions, and receding hairlines. Nephews weren't spared either. My uncles loved to tease my meager biceps and aspirations as a writer.

My cousin Henry checked a swath of typical teenage boxes: he enveloped himself in music and incense in his room, stressed about college, would spontaneously disappear to be with his friends, and Tindered at the dinner table. Dave and Henry were both overstressed, ardent Christians with endearingly facetious demeanors and a disinterest in Eastern voodoo—in other words, perfect test subjects. When I proposed a lesson in mindfulness meditation, they immediately accepted. To them, I was probably handing over a decade's worth of ammunition to tease me with.

Our first morning meditation was a flop. Eight minutes in, their ninety-pound black lab, Lacie, burst into the room to give each of us a sloppy kiss, throwing off our Zen before Henry and Dave had to head out. Thankfully, the boys were up for a mulligan the next morning. With the door barricaded and the faint aroma of cedarwood incense filling the room, we sat through fifteen minutes of silence.

To my pleasant surprise, after our first session, Dave immediately reported feeling measurable stress relief. After a few more sunrise sessions, my Aunt Laura pulled me aside after Dave departed. "I haven't seen my husband this calm in the morning in eighteen years. *What are y'all doing in there?*" When Dave had an early meeting the next morning, Henry volunteered to set his alarm back to join us in morning meditation—an act further befuddling his mother.

By the end of the week, both my uncle and cousin reported enhanced clarity, lowered stress, and simply feeling better throughout the day. After I left St. Louis, they continued the practice without me and still do to this day. Henry even bought his father a bonafide yoga square and cushion for his birthday, and the boys share a stash of incense from a nearby smoke shop.

Since my lessons with Dave and Henry, I've hosted meditation classes for a few hundred people of all ages and backgrounds. I have to admit I was nervous during the early sessions, bracing for the inevitable moment one of my students would whisper "this is stupid" to a neighbor or at the very least tell me that they felt no different after class. But that day never came. Everyone's brains seemed to be thanking them.

I also had veteran meditators join my classes to experience meditating in a group and the less common styles of meditation I teach (which we'll get to). Matt, thirty-one, is a graphic designer.

His job often demands endurance through long hours *and* consistent creativity. To prepare his mind to deliver this draining one-two punch, he meditates daily. "My mind used to be like an unclean room with thoughts all over the place," he says. "With meditation, it becomes more tidy. I can access and process thoughts more easily."

"I tend to be a high-strung person, always on the go," Ashley told me. She's a twenty-seven-year-old accountant with aspirations to open her own consulting business. The stresses of her daily load toss her mind around like a rowboat in a stormy sea, but she stays afloat using meditation. "The best way to describe the way I feel when I meditate is at peace. Time has stopped and there are no thoughts going through my brain."

So take it from us, Supreme Court Justice Stephen Breyer, Ford CEO Bill Ford, and rapper 50 Cent: meditation works.

But *why* does it work? After all, "go somewhere quiet and sit with your eyes closed" sounds like a lazy preschool punishment, not a neural cure-all.

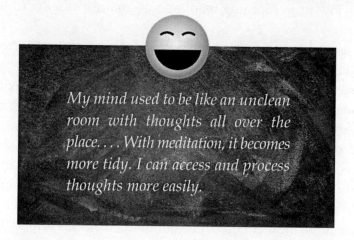

My mind used to be like an unclean room with thoughts all over the place. . . . With meditation, it becomes more tidy. I can access and process thoughts more easily.

The Dalai Lama, the spiritual figurehead of all Buddhism, calls meditation a "mind science." What do the lab coats have to say about that? Why do we lose track of time and experience out-of-body sensations when we meditate, and more importantly, can we *quantify* the benefits of routine practice?

The Science behind Mental Enemas

When my colleagues at Stanford and at other universities started researching meditation, most of us expected that meditation would help with stress levels. However, what many of us did not anticipate was the extent of the benefits the data ended up showing.

—Dr. Emma Seppälä

If I indulged my cold, calculating German side and tried to quantify the benefits of meditation with an exact percentage boost to happiness, I wouldn't be the first.

After fighting incredulity for years, *Nightline* anchor Dan Harris finally gave in to the power of meditation and began regular, devoted practice. But his love for it gave way to a new struggle. He had publicly rolled his eyes at meditation for so long that he couldn't find words to suddenly sell it to his friends, family, and colleagues. Soon, he found a way to get through to them: speak quantitatively.

"It makes me ten percent happier." (Hence the name of his book, *10% Happier*.)

Now, hearing that meditation is figuratively worth a dime of happiness may be a bit underwhelming. But let's remember that Dan is *not* a Millennial. In fact, he only began meditating *after* he'd been working his dream job for years and married the girl of his dreams. If meditation can make *his* life 10 percent better, imagine how powerful it'll be for us!

As someone still working on finding the dream girl and dream job, I'd say the mere practice of meditation alone makes me closer to 25 percent happier. **What's more important is that the clarity, focus, and calm it provides will *help* me discover more passions, find my dream girl, and succeed professionally, causing who knows how much more happiness.**

Moving to other parts of the body, studies have linked routine meditation practice to increased immune function, with subjects reporting a decrease in physical pain and even faster recovery from the flu. A 2012 study by the University of Wisconsin–Madison even found that beginner meditators missed 76 percent fewer work days due to seasonal illnesses.[1] In addition, researchers routinely find that meditators have significantly lowered depression, anxiety, and stress levels. They've also linked meditation to increased self-control, with improved emotional regulation and introspection. Lastly, meditators are simply smarter—compared to their control groups, they show an improved ability to multitask, recall memories, and think outside the box.

This all begs a simple question: *what the hell is going on up there when we meditate?* For the longest time, science has been able to list *outcomes* of meditation, but not explain *why* these benefits were happening from a neurological perspective. **With the advent of fMRIs, however, we can now watch the brain on meditation, and the wild activity we've seen puts REM sleep to shame.**

Taming the Brain

Neuroscientists have a scientific term loosely analogous to our subconscious. It's called our default mode network (DMN), and consists of brain areas related to reflection, introspection, and new memory consolidation. Because DMN activity increases when we're not focused on an activity, some neuroscientists liken it to the brain's "neutral gear."

Now, in an ideal world, our brains would operate like well-oiled engines, cleanly shifting gears between focus, reflection, focus, reflection, based on whether we were occupied with an activity or not. Concentrate in class, *shift*, digest what we've learned. Have a great time on a date, *shift*, reflect on the evening and decide whether we'd like to see them again.

The problem is, the world *isn't* ideal, and in the modern age we pound our brains with so much stimulation that the gearshift has gotten stuck in the middle. Neurologically speaking, our DMNs stay overactive while we're trying to focus, causing mind-wandering, stress, and loss of concentration. Try to listen in class, *daydream*. Try to focus on what our date is saying, *picture them naked*.

With overactive DMNs, we constantly worry about the past, future, and what others think of us instead of just focusing on the task at hand. Our naturally overactive DMNs are linked to anxiety, depression, ADHD, and severe psychological disorders.

So here's where meditation comes in. By isolating ourselves from all external stimuli for fifteen minutes, we're allowing our brains time to recalibrate our default mode networks. In 2011, Yale researchers measured this effect by performing fMRI scans on novice and lifetime meditators, noticing greatly decreased DMN activity both during and outside of meditation.[2] Meditation quite literally *tames* the subconscious. With calmer DMN activity, we're able to focus and reflect more easily, which indirectly reduces our stress levels. So if our focus and reflect gears are stuck, meditation applies the oil.

The engine lubrication isn't the only effect meditation has on the brain. Also in 2011, Harvard researchers discovered another measurable change that surely caused some dropped clipboards and a "holy Moses."

To further study the impact of meditation, researchers had nonmeditators begin meditating for an average of twenty-seven minutes per day across multiple sessions. After eight weeks, the researchers performed brain scans on both a control group and the group that had begun meditating. They found the novice meditators showed increased gray-matter density in the hippocampus, the area of the brain responsible for learning and memory, and a decrease in gray-matter density in the amygdala, known for anxiety and stress. **The meditators had permanently reduced their stress and increased their emotional control and memory processing.** "These people are not just feeling better because they're relaxing," says Dr. Sara Lazar, study author and psychology professor at Harvard Medical School.[3]

So in 2011, we learned that during meditation, not only does the brain *reprogram* itself, it literally *rebuilds* itself for long-term improvements to our cognitive functioning. "It is fascinating to see the brain's plasticity and that, by practicing meditation, we can play an active role in changing the brain and can increase our well-being and quality of life," writes Harvard researcher Britta Hölzel.[3]

"Yeah, my hippopotamus feels stronger already!" reports my Uncle Dave. "Seriously though, it's something I expect to do for the remainder of my days."

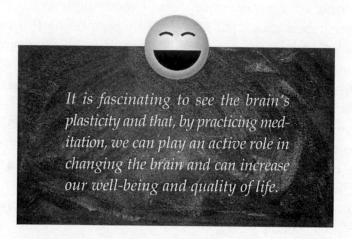

It is fascinating to see the brain's plasticity and that, by practicing meditation, we can play an active role in changing the brain and can increase our well-being and quality of life.

Our Next Public-Health Revolution

The two groundbreaking studies at Harvard and Yale have launched a frenzy of new research, as scientists now believe that, over longer terms, meditation will allow the brain to optimize other areas of itself. These new findings could explain why lifetime meditators show greater increases in health, intelligence, and success over novices just starting out; they've simply been building a better brain every day for years.

Armed with this knowledge, Dan Harris believes meditation will become the next public-health revolution. **"In the 1940s, if you told people you went running, they would say 'who's chasing you?' Right now, if you tell people you meditate . . . they look at you a little weird. That's going to change. Meditation is going to join the pantheon of no-brainers like exercise and brushing your teeth."[4]**

Now that we've covered the *what* and the *why*, let's get into the *how*. Are you ready for a better brain?

Your First Week of Meditation

Let's talk the basics. There are dozens of types of meditation, some of which we'll cover later, but the most popular form and the subject of most modern neurological research is the Buddhism-based mindfulness meditation. There's also the Hindu, chanting-based transcendental meditation, but this controversial form requires learning under a certified teacher and can cost thousands in course fees with mixed results.

We'll stick with mindfulness meditation for now since we know it works and it's free. Mindfulness meditation is the *chill out* version Siddhartha first practiced under the Bodhi Tree to achieve enlightenment, and has been the basic form of Buddhist meditation for millennia. Its pose and practice couldn't be simpler.

Your First Session

The Setting

Find a place at home or work where you can sit quietly for fifteen minutes free of interruptions like colleagues, noises, or flashing lights. Bedrooms or empty offices make great impromptu meditation halls. Make sure you have enough room to sit cross-legged on the floor.

The Pose

Next, find a cushion or pillow you can sit on that will raise your rear end about six inches off the ground. Pillows typically compress too much, but folding one in half works well. Sit on your pillow of choice and cross your legs. This is known quite simply as cross-legged pose. The iconic Padmasana, or lotus pose, with your legs crossed and feet pulled up onto the opposing thighs, is believed by some to provide slightly better posture and chi (spiritual energy) flow over basic cross-legged pose. If you're flexible enough, go for it, but otherwise lotus pose is unnecessary. Most of the monks of Magnolia Grove simply sit cross-legged for comfort.

Once you're seated, straighten your back and puff your chest out. If this feels strained or unnatural, congratulations, you'll be fixing your posture while you meditate, too!

Why not sit in a chair or lie down? In short, cross-legged and lotus poses maximize the flow of blood and oxygen to the brain to assist with the repairing process. They also improve your balance, posture, and help train small muscles in your back for better circulation. In early mornings, you're much less likely to drift off during cross-legged pose, as well.

Breathing

Place your hands on your knees and relax your shoulders. Before closing your eyes, practice slow breathing: *in for two seconds, hold for one second, out for three seconds.* Think to yourself, *In . . . out . . . in . . . out . . .* while you do it. Try to perform three deep breaths this way every minute or so during meditation. Otherwise, breathe normally. (For a neat, standalone deep-breathing exercise, see *ASAP Happiness*.)

Do I have to touch my fingers and say "ohm"? Touching your fingers is believed to further improve the flow of chi. Most of the monks I meditated with didn't bother. *Ohm* is a mantra, or sacred vibration (prayer), practiced during transcendental meditation. It's unnecessary for mindfulness meditation.

Switch your phone to airplane mode, set a timer for fifteen minutes, and close your eyes.

The key now is to let your subconscious run wild. Let the flurry of thoughts and memories that you've long suppressed come flooding into your lens of focus. Many may be bad or pointless; when it becomes too much, return to your breathing. *In two seconds . . . hold one second . . . out three seconds . . .* Return to letting your subconscious run wild for a bit, then back to your breathing. *In . . . out . . .*

Continue this pattern until the timer rings.

After Your First Session

Congratulations, you've completed your first meditation session! How'd it go?

All I did was think about stupid junk and awful memories for fifteen minutes, and now I'm even more stressed out!

This is to be expected. Even Dr. Mark Epstein, outspoken meditation advocate, concedes that the first few sessions "may actually raise your anxiety."[5] Remember, Mara is attacking you, or in neuroscientific terms, your default mode network is going haywire, and your brain will need a few more sessions to reprogram it. Think of meditation like exercise when you're out of shape—the first few sessions will feel tough, but you'll get better *and* feel the benefits once you're a few sessions in. Plus, from personal experience, the brain improves much more quickly from meditation than the body does from exercise.

The Rest of the Week

Good news! You're already past the worst session. Now, working your way up to Oprah's daily regimen doesn't take long. You don't have to suck at it like I've sucked at golf for ten years; with meditation, you'll get the hang of it pretty quickly.

All right, so we've knocked out our first fifteen minutes. Where to now? The monks of Magnolia Grove agree that forty-five-plus minutes is "quite difficult for many people," and while incredibly enlightening, isn't always practical outside of a monastic setting.

Sister Boi Nghiem has helped coach hundreds of Western yogis through their first weeks of meditation to develop lifelong habits. She and I have put together a Week 1 Meditation Schedule for beginners. Just like the practice, the regimen is extremely simple. It's the same schedule I used to help launch Uncle Dave, Henry, and others into lifelong habits, and I hope it does the same for you.

Day 1
1) Morning: 10 minutes

Day 2
2) Morning: 10 minutes

Day 3
3) Morning: 15 minutes

Day 4
4) Morning: 15 minutes
5) Evening: 10 minutes

Day 5
6) Morning: 15 minutes
7) Evening: 15 minutes

I know, it looks like a lot, but this of this beginning regimen as the best way to get over the "initial hump" like I did at the monastery. After you make it past day five, continue meditating for at least twelve minutes per day, every day. You can increase the frequency or time based on your personal preferences. Sometimes I only meditate for around five minutes for a "power nap" effect, while other times I go down for a full fifteen. Now that I've conquered Mara, I rarely feel the need to meditate twice in a day anymore, though I sometimes do for an even higher sense of calm and relaxation.

As for setting, once you're comfortable, begin experimenting with new meditation stations. My friends and I will often meditate in the sauna after a workout. My friend Sarah will pick a nice, sunny spot in the park to apply some oil and "meditan."

Now that we've covered mindfulness meditation, are there other meditation techniques we can try to trigger different effects?

The Boost: Your Meditation Toolkit

While we've been talking about meditation within the context of Buddhism, nearly every world religion practices some form of meditation. Monks, pastors, swamis, and saints alike have leveraged meditation to open their minds and become closer to their fellow practitioners, deities of choice, and themselves. Christian Saint Pio of Pietrelcina once wrote, "Through the study of books, one seeks God; by meditation one finds him."[6]

Oftentimes, especially in the West, meditation isn't even associated with a religion at all, but is exercised purely for benefits to body and mind. Once we've tamed our subconscious through basic meditation, we can better control our thoughts and try intermediate meditation techniques, which have us focusing on a specific object or idea for sweet new outcomes.

Through the study of books, one seeks God; by meditation one finds him.

In other words, think of regular meditation like upgrading your phone. The following techniques are like launching new apps. Together with mindfulness meditation, I collectively call them The Boost, and have given classes by the same name to a few hundred doctors, lawyers, students, nurses, entrepreneurs, ADHD patients, a pair of CNN producers, a professional racing driver, and a company of firemen. I'm often asked, "Do you also teach yoga?" to which I respond by trying to touch my toes, so they go, "Oh, guess not!"

Without further ado, let's begin The Boost.

Focus through Trataka: Meditate Like a Ninja

Trataka comes from the Sanskrit word for "gaze," and involves meditating by staring at a fixed point, typically the flame of a candle. In Hinduism, the practice is used to open the esoteric "third eye," promoting "siddhis," or psychic powers.

One group, however, used the technique for earthlier, more pragmatic purposes. The Japanese ninja were perhaps the most feared and revered special forces in the world before the Navy SEALs bagged bin Laden. By some historians' accounts, ninja were the most effective warriors of all time, defeating armies outnumbering them a hundred to one and assassinating warlords behind impenetrable fortresses.

Naturally these feats required superhuman focus, and lacking an Adderall prescription, the ninja routinely practiced Trataka. "It sharpens your senses," says Jinichi Kawakami, one of the last living ninja masters, "and with it, your sixth sense will develop naturally."[7]

Wait—isn't staring at fire bad for you? "This is not a problem due to the low light of the flame," optometrist Dr. John Bonsett-Veal assures us. "The sun is different and exceptionally dangerous by comparison."

A 2016 study published in *The Journal of Traditional and Complementary Medicine* pitted a control group against a group who'd practiced six to nine minutes of Trataka in a series of cognitive tests. The researchers noted a "significant difference" in performance between the two groups, noticing that "the Trataka technique increased the selective attention, cognitive flexibility, and response inhibition" of the subjects.[8]

So if mindfulness meditation is for relaxing and clearing our minds, Trataka is for getting things done with the efficiency of a ninja. For that reason, I find the two performed together turn me into Elon Musk; I get the clarity to think of creative solutions or ideas, and the focus to immediately take action. Trataka takes just a few minutes, so try a session right now.

Practice:

1) Assume your meditation pose.
2) Light a candle, and place it an arm's length away.
3) Focus on the flame for six minutes (with minimal blinking).

Flex Your Compassion through Metta

Metta, also known as loving-kindness or compassion meditation, is the practice of sending good vibes to people. Yup, I'm serious. Metta is nearly as old as Buddhism itself, first found in the *Pāli Canon*, the oldest known Buddhist text.

You practice Metta by sending silent well-wishes to loved ones, then people you're indifferent about, then if you're up for a challenge, people you're angry with, such as a significant other or friend. Metta challenges our sense of compassion—think of it like lifting weights at the gym, and focusing on the most difficult people is like adding weight.

If "sending good vibes" sounds a little too Burning Man for your taste, consider the underlying science. The practice of Metta flexes the insular cortex, the area of the brain responsible for empathy, and also lowers our production of cortisol. A 2012 study published in *Frontiers in Human Neuroscience* found that when compared to novice (eight weeks of practice) mindfulness meditators and a control group, novice compassion meditators exhibited an *increased* emotional response to negative stimuli, yet *fewer* symptoms of depression. They concluded that the curious results "may be explained by an increased capacity for compassion."[9]

As a novice Metta meditator myself, I've found that routinely exercising my compassion makes it much harder for others to piss me off, and easier to forgive those who do. Today, I practiced Metta by first focusing on Mama Butsch, then a new acquaintance, then my manipulative, dishonest ex. Yes, wishing *her* well is hard, but Metta has helped me forgive her and move on to new relationships.

I've also found that five minutes of Metta works *miracles* before facing rush-hour traffic, as the shot of empathy it provides suppresses road rage and allows for a more tranquil drive.

Practice:

1) Assume your meditation pose and close your eyes. No need for a timer.

2) Think of three people—a loved one, someone you're indifferent toward, and someone you're angry with.

3) One at a time, picture each of them sitting across from you.

4) In your head, imagine yourself saying that you wish them happiness, health, success, and love. Truly mean it, and visualize their reaction—perhaps a look of surprise, then a smile.

5) Picture the four of you together, and imagine your empathy for others spreading beyond your circle into the rest of the world.

Inject Perspective through Gratefulness Meditation

The basic concept of gratefulness meditation, predictably, is to reflect on people or things for which you're grateful, and soak in the instant happiness gratefulness provides. Mountains of research like a 2009 study in *The Journal of Personal and Social Psychology* directly link grateful thoughts to increased well-being, extraversion, and a positive outlook.[10] Simply put, "Growing evidence suggests that gratitude is a key element for sparking positive and sustained changes in individual well-being," writes Dr. Robert Emmons in *The Science of Subjective Well-Being*.[11]

Traditionally, gratefulness meditation involves thinking of five things for which you're grateful, but I found this totally underwhelming. So I added a few steps involving really picturing your life *without* those five wonderful things you enjoy now. Like Trataka, gratitude meditation takes just a few minutes, so try it right now.

Practice:

1) Assume your meditation pose and close your eyes. No need to set a timer.
2) For at least thirty seconds each, think of five things you're grateful for.
   a) Picture how each thing has improved your life.
   b) Picture your life without that thing.
3) After you've expressed gratitude for all five things, picture your life without *any* of them for a whole minute.
4) Finally, picture each of the five things being slowly gifted back to you.

Today, I felt thankful for my car, my loving parents, my access to food, my laptop, and being born in a free country. I then spent a minute visualizing life with no car, no parents, no laptop, hungry, and living in a third-world country. Then, having all of those things granted back to me in the span of a minute felt *awesome!*

My friend Shawn practices gratefulness meditation at least every other day, "especially when I'm in a bad mood or something bad happens." After five minutes, the fresh dose of perspective always improves his day. "It helps me remember, some things are not a big deal. Plus, it *keeps* working, and you start to think of more things you're thankful for!"

Train Body and Mind through Yoga: That Other Reason to Wear Yoga Pants

> *Yoga is not about tightening your ass. It's about getting your head out of it.*
>
> —Yoga teacher Eric Paskel

Yoga is a physical practice marrying meditation, exercise, and spirituality. Despite going back several millennia, yoga didn't exist in the West until Hindu revivalist Swami Vivekananda introduced it in the late nineteenth century, stating, "I have a message to the West as Buddha had to the East."[12] But due to a puritanical national mindset, disdain for foreign practices, and a lack of materials to make yoga pants, yoga remained unpopular in America for nearly a century.

Then, in the late twentieth century, advocates began downplaying yoga's overblown religious connotations and emphasizing its benefits to body and mind. The practice picked up steam in the early 2000s and exploded in popularity in the 2010s. Now, with 24 million practicing adults in America, yoga is more popular than golf.[13]

So what are the measurable benefits of practicing yoga? Do the scientific and fitness communities celebrate yoga's recent surge in popularity, or write it off as a passing, sensationalist fad?

The National Institute of Health considers yoga a valid exercise, stating its practice "might improve quality of life; reduce stress; lower heart rate and blood pressure; help relieve anxiety, depression, and insomnia; and improve overall physical fitness, strength, and flexibility."[14] Interestingly, the American College of Sports Medicine considers yoga to be a form of *stretching*, and lauds its enhancement of breath control and core strength.[15]

So what do we Millennials say? Do we consider yoga to be more than an excuse to shop at Lululemon?

Matt, twenty-five, is a successful entrepreneur who calls yoga one of the best habits of his life. "The focus on breath wakes and clears my mind, and every little muscle in my body gets some love."

Amanda, twenty-five, is an ever-stressed traveling consultant who relies on hot yoga to decompress. "It's hard to think about anything but what you're doing in the moment!"

"If you're writing about yoga in your book, you have to come to my class!" said my Aunt Laura. She was right, but I still protested.

"But I'm as flexible as a bowling ball."

She offered a sly smile. "What if I make Henry come with us?" Deal. At least that way I'd have another six-foot-three human tree to struggle alongside.

My takeaway from Aunt Laura's class and several others I attended is that yoga is more physically demanding than it looks. I frequent the gym and run the odd 5K, but I didn't need hot yoga to build up a sweat; regular yoga wrung me out. Poses like downward dog and python work and stretch countless muscles, some of which aren't otherwise conditioned during daily life. So for the uninitiated, the first class or two may wind you like a tough day at the gym or a long run. Once you build these muscles and can better control your breathing, however, yoga becomes pretty rewarding. The seemingly contradictory practices of meditation and exercise actually work pretty well together.

There are plenty of yoga styles out there, from the precision-based Lyengar to the heart-pumping Vinyasa. If you're interested in getting a general sampling, look for a Hatha class—an umbrella term for Western yoga, introducing bits from each style in a beginner-friendly environment.

What Can We Learn from Corpse Pose in Yoga?

Many yoga instructors consider Sivasana (corpse) to be the most important pose in yoga. As its name implies, corpse pose involves lying on our back, arms spread, and letting the floor support our whole body. Sivasana reveals areas where we may not have realized we were generating tension; once we release this tension, we enable ourselves to enter a calmer, more tranquil state. You can try Sivasana at home or anywhere it's acceptable to resemble a corpse, such as a war movie set or inside a white chalk line.

Boost Energy and Creativity through a Mediccino

In the last chapter we combined caffeine with power napping to help slingshot us into a productive afternoon. How does caffeine combine with *meditation*? Beautifully.

Our brain is the most fresh and clean in the morning, and a sunrise meditation session greatly amplifies that effect. Since caffeine takes fifteen to thirty minutes to affect the brain, if we drink a cup of coffee *just before* our morning meditation, we'll end the session with a surge of energy right when our minds are at their clearest. I've found that this brain-boosting one-two punch results in a spike in creative energy and a surge of motivation. I call it a *Mediccino* (I thought it sounded better than *Caffeitation*).

Is Meditation for You?

Yes. Yes, it is. If you've read this far and thought, *Meditation sounds cool, it's just not for me*, to that I'd say if you have a brain, meditation is for you. You have decades of life ahead, full of challenges and monumental decisions to make, and to reach your potential for happiness you'll need the most capable brain possible. If we're all navigating the sea of real life, meditation adds a compass, more oars, and calms the water. "The quality of our life depends on the quality of our mind," writes Sri Sri Ravi Shankar, the closest we have to a modern-day Gandhi. Adds Stanford researcher Dr. Emma Seppälä, "When I started meditating, I did not realize it would also make me healthier, happier, and more successful."(16)

If you don't take it from them, consider words from my friend Chip. In college, Chip kicked ass on the lacrosse team, joined a popular fraternity, and could shotgun two beers at once. He was about as far from a monk as conceivably possible; I once called him "a human broverdose."

Yet underneath the fratty armor, Chip was a sweet and sensible guy. The untimely passing of a teammate reminded him that "life is very fragile, and very short. In that moment I realized I wasn't living a fulfilled life. It was artificial happiness combined with *huge* amounts of anxiety that I had no control over." Like me, Chip realized his happiness was draining through a gash in his psyche, and partying was like "applying morphine, when I really needed stitches."

Seeking long-term repair, Chip picked up a copy of Eckhart Tolle's *The Power of Now*, which inspired him to attend group-meditation sessions on campus. Each time, after training his brain and facing his negative emotions head on, "I'd get up and walk away in a completely different state of mind."

Five years later, Chip feels more at ease on a daily basis, working at a job he loves with a company he loves. Despite the demands of his work and social life, he never lets a day slip by without a fifteen-minute mindfulness meditation session.

"Life is a skill. If you want to learn how to live a happy life, you *have* to put effort in developing yourself. Meditation has been the key to understanding those flaws in myself, *and* the key to fixing them."

So if you haven't started meditating, take fifteen minutes right now to jump back to the section Your First Week of Meditation. Then, play around with some of the other techniques; just be sure to keep practicing mindfulness meditation for at least twelve minutes every day. Very soon you'll start feeling and experiencing life with a better brain.

If you're interested in learning each of the five techniques in a one-on-one or group session with me, I'd love to have you as a student! Please visit my website, www.chrisbutsch.com.

After twenty minutes of meditation this morning (six minutes of Trataka, followed by a fourteen-minute mediccino), I played through a few *Lumosity* games to test my new brain. Before my monastic adventure, I'd maxed out at a score of 1,311. Today, I scored 1,704.

Aside from building a better brain, meditation simply unlocks too much happiness to be ignored. So I implore you, don't move on to the final chapter of this book until you've offered your hard-working brain some respite. I promise, it will thank you.

References:

1) Barrett, Bruce, Mary S. Hayney, Daniel Muller, David Rakel, Ann Ward, Chidi N. Obasi, Roger Brown et al. "Meditation or exercise for preventing acute respiratory infection: a randomized controlled trial." *The Annals of Family Medicine* 10, no. 4 (2012): 337-346.

2) Brewer, Judson A., Patrick D. Worhunsky, Jeremy R. Gray, Yi-Yuan Tang, Jochen Weber, and Hedy Kober. "Meditation Experience Is Associated with Differences in Default Mode Network Activity and Connectivity." *Proceedings of the National Academy of Sciences* 108, no. 50 (December 13, 2011): 20254–59. Accessed April 22, 2016. doi:10.1073/pnas.1112029108. http://www.pnas.org/content/108/50/20254.short.

3) Hölzel, Britta K., James Carmody, Mark Vangel, Christina Congleton, Sita M. Yerramsetti, Tim Gard, and Sara W. Lazar. "Mindfulness practice leads to increases in regional brain gray matter density." *Psychiatry Research: Neuroimaging* 191, no. 1 (2011): 36–43.

4) Big Think. "Dan Harris: Hack Your Brain's Default Mode with Meditation." YouTube. August 19, 2014. https://www.youtube.com/watch?v=FAcTIrA2Qhk.

5) Barbor, Cary. "The Science of Meditation." May 01, 2001. Accessed April 25, 2016. https://www.psychologytoday.com/articles/200105/the-science-meditation.

6) Kelly, Liz. *The Rosary: A Path into Prayer*. Chicago: Loyola University Press, US, 2004.

7) Peiter, Sebastian and John Wate. *Ninja: Shadow Warriors*. Directed by John Wate. UK: The Smithsonian Channel, 2012. Film.

8) Raghavendra, B. R. and Prashanth Singh. "Immediate Effect of Yogic Visual Concentration on Cognitive Performance." *Journal of Traditional and Complementary Medicine* 6, no. 1 (January 1, 2016): 34–36. Accessed May 1, 2016. doi:10.1016/j.jtcme.2014.11.030. http://ac.els-cdn.com/S2225411014000443/1-s2.0-S2225411014000443-main.pdf?_tid=96a60206-8070-11e6-b40c-00000aab0f6c&acdnat=1474513353_357d8e22b0758c9b6443a137fb884a38.

9) Desbordes, Gaëlle, Lobsang T. Negi, Thaddeus W. W. Pace, B. Alan Wallace, Charles L. Raison, and Eric L. Schwartz. "Effects of Mindful-Attention and Compassion Meditation Training on Amygdala Response to Emotional Stimuli in an Ordinary, Non-Meditative State." *Frontiers in Human Neuroscience* 6 (November 1, 2012). doi:10.3389/fnhum.2012.00292.

10) Emmons, R. A., & McCullough, M. E. (2003). "Counting blessings versus burdens: an experimental investigation of gratitude and subjective well-being in daily life." *Journal of Personality and Social Psychology*, 84(2), 377.

11) Emmons, R. A. (2008). "Gratitude, subjective well-being, and the brain." *The Science of Subjective Well-Being*, 469–489.

12) Thomas, Wendell. *Hinduism Invades America (1930).* New York, NY, United States: Kessinger Publishing Co, 2003.

13) Painter, Kim. *Ancient Practice of Yoga Now a Growth Industry. USA TODAY.* March 3, 2015. http://www.usatoday.com/story/news/nation/2015/03/01/yoga-health-fitness-trends/23881391/.

14) "Yoga: In Depth." May 2, 2008. Accessed April 22, 2016. https://nccih.nih.gov/health/yoga/introduction.htm.

15) Caplan, Mindy. "Yoga: An Asset for Personal Training Professionals." February 19, 2013. Accessed April 22, 2016.

http://certification.acsm.org/blog/2013/february/diver
sify-your-clients-workouts-with-yoga.

16) Seppala, Emma M. "20 Scientific Reasons to Start Meditating Today." September 11, 2013. Accessed September
25, 2016.
https://www.psychologytoday.com/blog/feeling-
it/201309/20-scientific-reasons-start-meditating-
today.

Chapter 5 Takeaways:

- By calming overactive areas of the brain and shuffling around gray matter, meditation provides a way for the brain to optimize itself with increased short- and long-term performance.
- Alternative techniques like Trataka, Metta, Gratitude, and Mediccino amplify our focus, compassion, happiness, and creativity, respectively.
- The practice of meditation takes time and discipline to integrate into our daily routine, but the payoff is tremendous as it provides long-lasting upgrades to our cognition.

Coming Up in Chapter 6:

- Mindfulness: repairing our relationship with the present moment
- The basics of mindfulness, as taught by a sassy, twenty-four-year-old Buddhist monk
- Flow: the most powerful natural high we can achieve, and how to achieve it more often

Chapter 6
Mindfulness: Moment-to-Moment Happiness

*Life consists only of moments, nothing more than that. So
if you make the moment matter, it all matters.*
> —Harvard professor and
> mindfulness expert Ellen Lange

I'll confess to having tried Adderall. I did it a handful of times
in college when in a pinch and a few more times on the job so I
could work a few Saturdays without going postal. Maybe a dozen
times in total. I stuck with the light stuff, five to ten milligrams
max at a time, but the effect was unbelievable.

Adderall is a low-grade amphetamine that releases dopamine
and sharpens your focus. The best way to describe the sensation
is that everything becomes more engaging. Class, meals, TV, and
friends all just seem *way* more interesting, so you're naturally
more attentive and focused. On Adderall, you're extremely in
tune with the present moment. The downside is that you lose your
appetite, stay up all night, and risk an amphetamine addiction.
Most people with a prescription seem to hate the stuff.

I bring up Adderall and risk having one of you try it (don't be
a shortsighted bing-bong like me) because it's the closest thing I
can think of to living in a state of mindfulness. Only mindfulness
is better on every level, and you don't need a prescription—just a
little practice.

Our Desperate Need for Mindfulness

What lies behind you and what lies in front of you, pales in comparison to what lies inside of you.
—Ralph Waldo Emerson

Imagine that if every time you sat down for lunch, all you could do is worry whether you had the right thing for breakfast and daydream about what you'd be having for dinner. *Are Honey Nut Cheerios really that healthy? I could go for some dope hot-wings tonight . . . no, salmon . . . no, hot wings . . .* Soon, lunch hour ends and you've barely touched your food. Now imagine doing this during every meal, every day. Eventually you'd starve, always thinking about other meals, never enjoying the food right in front of you!

Sadly, most of us go through life this way, perpetually plagued by thoughts of the past and concerns of the future, out of sync with the present moment. My thoughts used to constantly bounce between past and present like a ping-pong ball. *That indie DJ I met last week was such an elitist douche . . . I wonder how long I'll have to work before I get promoted . . .*

As Americans, our detachment from the present moment is becoming increasingly evident as our national stress and anxiety levels creep up to alarming levels. According to the American Psychological Association, in 2015 all four living generations reported increased stress levels between 2014 and 2015, with young adults reporting the greatest spike. In 2014, 36 percent of Millennials reported increased stress levels from the year before. In 2015, it was 45 percent.[1]

That means that *half* of us are getting more stressed out each year! What's causing all of this hair-pulling anxiety?

The Millennial's Quest for Stress Relief

It's no coincidence that our inflating stress levels coincide with a greater percentage of our generation entering the workforce each year. As we become acquainted to our new jobs, our bosses tell us how to access the Wi-Fi, what to bring to meetings, and when to submit expense reports, but never do they say, "And here's how to deal with the stress maelstrom heading your way." **As work or grad school ramps up, each day becomes a battle with ego depletion and continued stress. We're certainly not armed for this battle, and even worse, we're picking up the wrong weapons.**

According to the APA, as compared to other generations we're most likely to battle stress by going online, eating, and playing video games. But as we've learned, battling stress with these activities is like battling a zombie with silly string: we may slow it down, but once it starts consuming us, we'll wish we'd gone with a different strategy.

We've already covered several of the most effective strategies for battling stress; meditation, exercise, and adequate sleep are your crossbows and katanas for the stress apocalypse. But here's a question we often don't consider: how do we *prevent* stress in the first place?

The answer lies in reengaging the present moment and training ourselves to slow down and enjoy the meal of life.

Mindfulness: Reengaging the Present Moment

The practice of mindfulness is all about getting us back in touch with the present moment. Through mindfulness, we refocus our attention on the here and now so we can give every moment as close to 100 percent as possible—every conversation, every meal, every activity. Mindfulness is living in the here and now as we're meant to, whether it's enjoying the gentle caress of a breeze, treasuring the company of an old friend, or dominating work while we're in the office.

Simply put, mindfulness is respect for the present moment. It generates gratefulness, efficiency, and focus. Over time, it snowballs into higher quality and quantity of relationships, rapid personal growth, better grades, and kicking ass at your job.

Signs for Magnolia Grove say *Buddhist Monastery and Mindfulness Training Center*. This dual label is for the benefit of the layman because these terms are synonymous, like *St. Pius Church and Prayer Community* or *Taco Bell: Mystery Mexican and Instant Regret Center*. Mindfulness is a pillar of the Buddhist practice; the monks live in a state of constant mindfulness, approaching every activity and interaction with the upmost respect and attention.

So how does constant mindfulness manifest itself in real life? How can you tell that the monastery is filled with Jedi of mindfulness?

Facilities are *obsessively* clean, and the symmetry and precision in the gardens rival that of the White House lawn. The new four-bedroom dorm the monks are building (with very limited outside help) rockets toward completion as the monks, young and old, paint, caulk, and saw with silent smiles. I've never seen anything like it on fifty Habitat for Humanity sites I've worked on, even when most of the volunteers were professionals. With tool belts wrapped around their robes, the monks shingled the entire roof in *hours* when it would've taken professionals days.

Mindfulness spilled into their culinary practices, as well. A single whiff in the kitchen assuaged your author's anxiety over the all-vegan diet. The monks prepared the food with such precision and perfection that the taste would've rendered Gordon Ramsey speechless.

Shortly after, I began my mindfulness journey with the monks by practicing mindful eating. The monks ate in total silence, save for the click of chopsticks and slurp of noodles. They carefully wrap multiple ingredients into each bite and chew slowly, occasionally putting their utensils down to contemplate their last bite. As Sister Ocean would explain, the application of mindfulness to eating provides a wealth of physical, mental, and spiritual benefits. Eating slowly, the monks can better adhere to *hara hachi bun me* and gauge when they're 80 percent full. They also take time to be grateful for each bite; they're thankful for the farmers, plants, herbs, and cooks who all came together to provide this nourishment for their bodies. While chewing, they take a moment to soak in every flavor, extracting the richness from each ingredient. The mindful meals with the monks were among the healthiest and happiest I'd ever had.

Before then, I couldn't recall the last time I had a deliberately mindful meal. I harkened back to a particularly hectic day at Epic when I furiously sporked fried rice into my face while speed-walking to my next meeting. Or even my last mindless meal before I met the monks: bear-clawing eight dollars worth of Wendy's down my gullet while driving across the Alabama-Mississippi border, dusting chicken nugget crumbs off of my sweatshirt.

The monks' message during mindful eating was clear. To echo the lessons from the food chapter, we need to stop having meaningless one-night stands with food and begin nurturing a loving and respectful relationship. By halving my usual eating pace and contemplating each bite, I soaked in the food's flavor and even forgot about my typically carnivorous tendencies. My stomach signaled my 80 percent fullness on time, so I left the table with double the usual energy. My gratefulness for the meal boosted my mood, and lastly, my focus allowed me to enjoy the meal from beginning to end, unfettered by worries of the past or present.

It occurred to me that the way I had been mindlessly eating food for years was like fast-forwarding through a good movie; I'd been blasting through the whole reason I sat down and got up with a hint of nausea.

Obviously, it's not practical to eat half-speed *all* the time, especially since your friends will still eat at a speedy pace, but even just slowing down *a bit* and taking the occasional pause will work wonders for our bodies and minds.

Mindful eating would forever change how I approach meals. The monks' next mindful challenge for me would forever change how I approach stressful situations.

Chainsaw Mindfulness

As I'd learn firsthand, the best way to prep for mindfulness is to meditate. By clearing out the junk and lubricating our thought process, we greatly increase our capacity for focus and distraction-free thinking. "Meditation and mindfulness go hand in hand—one makes way for the other, and back and forth," Sister "D" would explain to me.

After several hours of collective meditation and various mindfulness practices such as walking, cleaning, and even teeth-brushing, the monks put me through my most demanding mindfulness test yet. Lightning had bisected a nearby, century-old oak tree, and the monks were interested in salvaging the fallen half. They asked me to apply some "Western muscle" and a nearby farmer's chainsaw to make some firewood for the sisters' dorm.

The odds were not in my favor; the tree had fallen on a slippery slope, my aid was an aging Vietnamese monk who communicated via wild, unintelligible hand signals, and the chainsaw didn't work. I gave the ripcord one last fruitless tug, but it was hopeless. I then raised my gaze to the monk, who waved his arms like a sassy traffic cop. *Ugh.*

All right, mindfulness muscle, time for a workout.

The monk and I began by meditating to calm and clear our minds. I then decided we should head to the monks' toolshed to find some face protection and tools. The monk and I took apart the chainsaw to find the internals choked with woodchips and dust. We each instinctively blew on the sawdust, launching it into each other's faces, coughing and laughing as we put the pieces back together. With some gas, oil, and another good tug to the ripcord, the chainsaw roared to life.

Sectioning the tree proved to be a dangerous puzzle in itself. The tree had fallen on its side, unevenly distributing its weight across the branches like a petrified, nine-legged beast. Without careful planning, we could cut the wrong limb at the wrong time, bringing the several-ton tree crashing down on us. Plus, my footing often disagreed with the dew-soaked grassy slope. If I was training to be a Jedi of mindfulness, this would be like my first lightsaber battle, with similar risk of self-dismemberment.

Thankfully, our liberated minds helped us strategize our approach. The monk sat atop the tree, applying weight so I could find the center of mass and predict how certain branches would react if others were cut. We ordered the limbs, then I spun up the chainsaw. Through the spray of woodchips and clouds of smoke, we safely severed the beast to pieces. The only surprise for the rest of the afternoon came when the old monk solicited a fist bump.

Several hours later, through the art of chainsaw mindfulness, we had turned half of an ancient oak into a beautiful pile of firewood—all forty fingers and toes intact.

Years ago, I never would've been able to get the job done without a grisly mishap, frustration, or even immediately giving up at the dead chainsaw. Had I artificially induced focus through caffeine or Adderall, I may have had the *concentration* necessary to complete the lumberjack jigsaw puzzle, but not the clarity and calm. Only meditation and mindfulness could provide all three, and by first strategizing and then freeing ourselves of distractions, we stayed mindful throughout the job.

This time, mindfulness hadn't just sped up or made a task more enjoyable; it had predicated success altogether.

Following my monastic adventures, I began applying mindfulness to *everything*: driving, eating, cooking, writing, partying, washing my car, watching *Archer*, even having conversations. I now understand why it helped the monks build a house so freakishly fast; living in mindfulness makes every moment better. In short, it makes good times feel longer and more enriching, and bad times go by more efficiently and painlessly.

Which begs the question: what does the scientific community have to say about this seemingly super-powered lifestyle?

The Science of Mindfulness

Measuring moment-to-moment happiness presents a tremendous challenge to researchers, since they can't just sneak up behind us with MRI machines while we're working or looking into our lover's eyes. But Harvard researcher Matt Killingsworth found a novel way.

He asked fifteen thousand people from eighty countries to report their happiness at random intervals, sometimes moment-to-moment, and found that we're most happy while we're fully engaged in an activity. When we daydream or lose focus even a bit, our happiness dips.

But what if we're sitting in rush-hour traffic and daydreaming about puppies and Pinkberry? Nope. "As it turns out, people are less happy when they're mind-wandering no matter *what* they're doing." So the more we focus on the present moment, the happier we become. **Focus and happiness are directly related.** "If mind-wandering were a slot machine, it would be like having a chance to lose fifty dollars, twenty dollars, or one dollar. You'd never want to play."

Still, maybe our minds are just wandering *because* we're already unhappy? Again, nope! Killingsworth's 650,000 data points suggest, "Mind-wandering very likely seems to be an actual cause, not merely a consequence, of unhappiness."[2]

So our brains love to focus *even if* it's on something unpleasant, like watching our boss's vacation slide show or our roommate failing at our favorite video game. But why is that? Why does our brain prefer to focus on an unpleasant activity rather than daydream and ignore it? Well, the answer lies in another way we as a species are evolving behind schedule.

"Our brain is wired to pay attention more frequently, with more veracity, to what's negative," writes Dr. Elisha Goldstein, author of *Uncovering Happiness*. Basically, we're predisposed to think about nasty things that could cause us emotional or physical pain "because as a human race, we're wired to survive, not be happy . . . This doesn't mean that the good things in life aren't happening. We're just not wired to pay attention to them."[3]

So even if we're focusing on something unpleasant, our minds would rather learn about how this *doesn't* make us happy than fantasize about things that *do*. "Mindfulness provides us with awareness and the opportunity to take wise actions to further balance this negativity bias. This is an evolution of an enduring happiness," says Dr. Goldstein.

To summarize thus far, mindfulness, or engaging the present moment, provides focus, calm, stability, and happiness, enhancing everyday activities like commuting, cleaning, cooking, conversing, and canoeing. When we mindfully engage more complex tasks like studying or strategizing, we greatly increase our chances of success. Lastly, mindfulness overcomes our evolutionary predisposition to focus on the negative, blocking out noise and training our minds to extract happiness from everything we do and identify which activities make us the happiest.

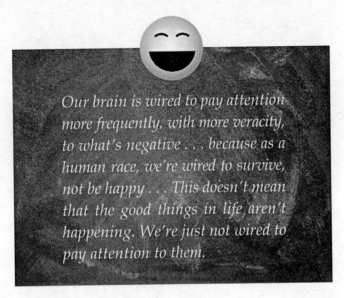

Our brain is wired to pay attention more frequently, with more veracity, to what's negative . . . because as a human race, we're wired to survive, not be happy . . . This doesn't mean that the good things in life aren't happening. We're just not wired to pay attention to them.

But overcoming our perennial paranoia sounds a little daunting. Thankfully, like with meditation, the practice of mindfulness is elegantly simple.

Your Mindfulness Training

The skill to be fully present to extract maximum joy and enrichment out of every moment is a no-brainer. But is it really possible to just *switch on* an Adderall-like effect in our brains like a superpower?

I threw this question to Brother Harmony, a nine-year veteran of mindfulness practices with a personality shattering the stoic monk stereotype. Born in Vietnam and raised in Germany, Brother Harmony spoke perfect English, called me "bro," and despite the weight of his winter robes, could launch a football with a perfect spiral. One frosty morning, when I showed up to walking meditation in my favorite leather jacket and aviator sunglasses, he remarked, "Ah, Brother Terminator is among us!"

"Bro Harmo," as we'd affectionately dubbed him, was a regular music-bumping, hoodie-wearing teenager in Germany when he first discovered mindfulness. One day he spotted a throng of Buddhist monks slowly meandering through Berlin's financial district carrying loose grins and calm demeanors. The tranquil orange troop stood out in near-comical contrast to the hurried blur of black, blue, and gray suits around them.

Soon-to-be Brother Harmony watched as they rounded a street corner, gazing in quiet wonder toward the sky and skyscrapers, less in awe than simply under a mysterious spell of bliss. "Everybody around them walked," he recalls. "The difference is they were more present and happy."

So back in '07, Bro Harmo investigated the nearby monastery with his mother, fell in love, and received his family's blessing to join the monkhood. After living in Plum Village Monastery in France throughout his teens and early twenties, he moved to Magnolia Grove, and now acts as an unofficial emissary between the monastery's young visitors and ancient practices.

Naturally, he was the perfect target for my next question. For us hyperstimulated, hyperstressed Millennials, the present moment is miles away. How can we hope to reengage it?

"Mindfulness is a technique everybody can learn," he says. "It's increasing the gratitude and appreciation for what you have in the present moment. It's helped me be aware of my life more, of what I can do." *But doesn't living in a monastery make mindfulness a little . . . easier?* Not as much as you'd think. Bro Harmo still deals with many of the basic human problems we do, like having roommates.

"Let's say someone calls me lazy. If I'm not mindful, I'll get pissed off. If I'm mindful, I'll remember not to create further suffering for me or others."

So how do we train to be more mindful every day? The practice of mindfulness, he explains, begins with some prep work.

First, minimize pleasures and distractions. Think of your mind as hungry. "When you eat, you satisfy your physical hunger. When you do things mindfully, you satisfy your *mental* hunger," he says. Pleasures are like mental junk food. "If you just continue drinking, smoking, having sex, and playing video games, you're trying to avoid suffering and difficulty with yourself. You will feel satisfied, but only for a period of time."

Another drawback to having too many pleasures in our lives is that we tend to daydream about them. Even when we're not actively putting Doritos in our body, we tend to think about them, hindering our mindfulness. So as we transition to lives of true happiness over pleasure, living in mindfulness becomes more natural.

Next, meditate. In addition to our daily practice, an ad hoc session provides a boost of mindfulness just before challenging activities. This neural pregame provides a wealth of benefits; first, we'll preemptively process our buzzing thoughts so they won't distract us during our task. Next, we'll enter our activity with lower stress. Lastly, we'll feel a boost in happiness, entering our next activity with a more positive outlook.

What if we're short on time, or aren't somewhere convenient to meditate? "Try two minutes of mindful breathing—in for two seconds, hold for one, out for three. Think: *breathing in, I'm aware I'm breathing in . . . Breathing out, I'm aware I'm breathing out."*

Lastly, show respect for the present moment. That may sound a little hippy-dippy, but if we think of the present moment as a good friend, we're often pretty rude to it. Checking our phones, pulling up Instagram, zoning out . . . a *real* friend would probably go, "Dude, really? I'm right here!" But the present moment doesn't have a voice, so it's up to our own volition to remember that focusing equals happiness.

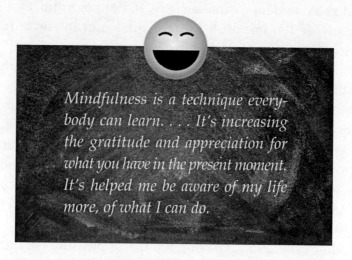

Mindfulness is a technique everybody can learn. . . . It's increasing the gratitude and appreciation for what you have in the present moment. It's helped me be aware of my life more, of what I can do.

Keeping our phones off the table and tucked away and closing our laptops are instant, easy ways to return a big percentage of our attention back to the present moment. We can even be mindful while on our laptops by keeping active programs and Internet tabs to an absolute minimum.

If we sense ourselves losing focus, Bro Harmo offers an ancient Buddhist trick to reengage mindfulness: simply close your eyes for a few seconds, breathe deeply, and give thanks for your current surroundings. The monks also do this at the top of every hour and any time they hear a bell. One morning, an old alarm on my phone went off, and as I fumbled to shut it up, the monks fell silent and smiled, giving thanks for the present moment.

From personal experience, I find maintaining mindfulness becomes tough when I suddenly think of a to-do or a funny picture or video I want to show a friend. In both cases I'm tempted to pull out my phone or laptop. But unless we have Zen-like discipline, our gadgets often hit us with an open-palm slap of distractions, ripping us from the present moment. Even if you ignore your notifications, they'll still sit in the back of your mind as you try to continue your conversation. So when considering pulling your phone out during times of mindfulness, ask yourself: is it worth it?

As for jotting down thoughts distraction-free, the monks carry around small notepads and pens. I've seen plenty of businessmen and entrepreneurs do the same. Eminem calls his fervent notetaking "stacking ammo."[4]

So that's mindfulness: It's a switch precipitated by some prep work, and with practice, we'll rarely need to "switch" into mindfulness at all. "You need to create a habit," Brother Harmony says. "It's not just one day or two days, it's day-by-day." Minimize your distractions, discipline your phone usage, reduce your reliance on pleasures, and use deep breathing to lasso yourself back to the present. On a moment-to-moment basis, treat the present moment like an old friend, and pay it the respect and attention it deserves.

So as Bro Harmo and I mindfully toss the football back and forth, is anyone in the outside world actually practicing this stuff, like meditation and yoga? Or is the practice not *quite* scientific enough to hold Western attention?

Modern Mindfulness

While mindfulness hasn't quite settled into corporate vernacular like meditation has, the practice has penetrated equally as many Fortune 500 offices. Goldman Sachs, Blackrock, and Bank of America all have mindfulness training programs, as well as Aetna, Adobe Systems, and General Mills. Google has an entire *division* devoted to mindfulness training called Search Inside Yourself, helmed by Zen master Chade-Meng Tan, formerly Google's "Jolly Good Fellow."

In his book *Mindful Work*, author David Gelles offers an inside look at how mindfulness changes a Western professional's mind over the long term. "All mindfulness is doing is trying to get us more attuned to the thoughts, emotions, and sensations that we're experiencing. Now, people have reported that their mindfulness practice made them more sensitive to things like environmental concerns and the conditions of factory workers." Today, more companies are perking up to Zen-centric training, since the benefits of mindfulness are becoming *quantifiable.* **"When Aetna rolled out its big mindfulness program, after the first full year, they saw out-of-pocket healthcare costs go down . . . it wasn't a drag on the bottom line, it was a boost to it."**[5]

But wait a second—how do these corporations design *entire programs* around mindfulness when Bro Harmo just taught us the essentials in a few minutes?

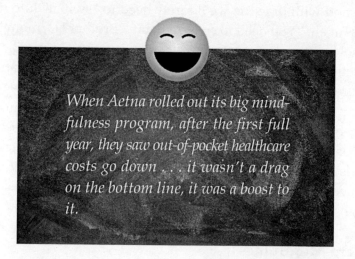

When Aetna rolled out its big mind-fulness program, after the first full year, they saw out-of-pocket healthcare costs go down . . . it wasn't a drag on the bottom line, it was a boost to it.

Many of these companies combine mindfulness with meditation training, as well as heavily delve into the neuroscience of it all so corporate curmudgeons don't write it off as a traveling spiritual sideshow. Underneath the charts and well-produced videos, the basics are mostly the same. For example, neuroscientist and Search Inside Yourself instructor Philippe Goldin begins his mindfulness course by saying, "Turn off your computers and cell phones and just be present."[6] Sound familiar?

When I first began reconnecting with the present moment, it wasn't too happy to see me. *Dude, where have you BEEN? We haven't talked since, like, middle school!* But tensions eased quickly as I began giving it more respect and attention. Through mindfulness and reconciliation with the present moment, my rate of writing has increased, driving is more enjoyable, meals are tastier, and my real friends have even called out my sharper listening skills.

So I urge you: make peace with *your* present moment.

A Quick Trick for Fighting Bad Memories

Mindfulness has also helped me battle and conquer an ancient foe that we all have in common: the tendency for our brains to replay awkward or negative memories. This mental masochism is equally devious and hard to overcome. In the words of comedian Mo Rocca, "I tried to put my phone down once . . . but then I was forced to feel my feelings for over twenty minutes per day, which I was not ready to do."[7]

The worst wave of negativity came when I used to lie in bed for too long without falling asleep. Then, unpleasant thoughts and memories would emerge from the recesses of my psyche like a street gang from the shadows to push me around. *Remember that time you blew a snot bubble in front of your crush in fifth grade? What a dork! How about that time you broke Becca's chair and never paid for it? She probably hates you! She's probably sitting in bed hating you right now and there's nothing you can do about it!*

In 2001, Dr. Raj Raghunathan, a researcher with the University of Texas at Austin, led a study finding that around 60 to 70 percent of our spontaneous thoughts are negative. He calls this phenomenon "negativity dominance," and postulates that the human brain tends to stay negative partly because it's more useful to our survival.[8]

I used to drown out pesky memories and bad thoughts with music or movies. Then, I discovered two better ways: one spiritual, one scientific.

The first tip comes from Thich Nhat Hanh, and it goes like this: Imagine your past self as a small child, and just give yourself a hug. Try comforting yourself with reassuring words and forgive yourself for whatever you did. Even if it was last week, your past self is just a child who needs your assurance and comfort.

The second tip springs from science. A 2010 study published in *Social Cognitive and Affective Neuroscience* found that refocusing on different aspects of the memory, such as clothes or people in the room, helps the brain recategorize the nasty memories from emotion-based to data-based, the latter of which are much more easily forgotten. I've used this trick to erase plenty of unpleasant memories. I'd provide examples, but I seriously can't remember any. *Awesome.*

The news gets even better, because mindfulness opens the door to radical periods of *extreme* focus, a state of mind so powerful it's set world records, built man's greatest accomplishments, and even helped us fall in love. And while such bold claims are usually found in Scientology propaganda or Kanye's autobiography, we know they're true in this case because many of us have experienced this state of mind before . . .

Flow: Engaging Super [Insert Your Name]!

At age thirty, science writer Steven Kotler was diagnosed with Lyme disease. Bedridden and operating at 10 percent for nearly three years, Steven could soon no longer take medication because his stomach lining had bled out. His hope equally eroded, he decided to commit suicide. He wasn't depressed; he just felt selfish and useless burdening his friends and family any further.

On his secretly planned final day, Steven's friends dragged him out of bed to go surfing. "It was a ridiculous request . . . but I figured, what the hell, what's the worst that can happen? *I can always kill myself tomorrow.*"[9]

Despite his sapped strength, Steven made it to Sunset Beach and, with his friends' support, paddled out to sea. Soon, he even managed to catch a wave. Then a few more. After a while, he "entered another dimension . . . time had slowed to an absolute crawl." And here's where things get weird: "The strangest thing is, I felt great. I felt better than I had felt in years . . . I felt that thrum of possibility."

Naturally, the physical exertion on his sickly body ended up immobilizing him for a few weeks, but the moment he mustered a modicum of strength, he hitchhiked back to the beach with his board. After a few waves, he achieved the mysterious euphoria once again.

Steven chased this feeling for six months. Soon, he was able to surf more frequently, noticing a drastic shift in his daily health and attitude. "I went from ten-percent functionality to eighty-percent functionality." No medication, just surfing.

"What the hell is going on? I'm a science writer, a rational materialist. I don't *have* quasi-mystical experiences . . ."

While catching waves, Steven was experiencing a neurological state called flow. Flow has other names: athletes call it "getting in the zone," musicians and dancers call it "getting in the groove" or "playing in the pocket." Commonly referred to as "the optimal state of consciousness," flow occurs when our skills match the challenge of an activity and our brains engage a hyperfocused, euphoric state. Flow is the most powerful natural high we can achieve, and compared to *un*natural highs, during flow we feel *and perform* at our best. Because of this, many scientists believe flow underpins most gold medals, achievements in arts and science, and even successes in business.

Flow as a concept has existed in Eastern cultures for over 2,300 years. Taoist scholar Chuang Tzu coined the term *Yu*, roughly translated as "walking without touching the ground," to describe the mystical euphoria one can achieve when attention is completely focused on an activity.[10] We've been "getting in the zone" for millennia, but only recently has science begun dissecting what "the zone" really is.

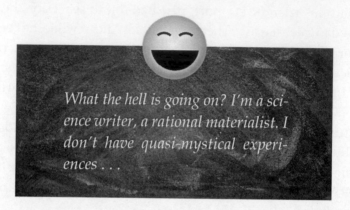

What the hell is going on? I'm a science writer, a rational materialist. I don't have quasi-mystical experiences . . .

By interviewing thousands of sculptors, writers, dancers, businesspeople, soldiers, and scientists, positive psychologist Mihaly Csikszentmihalyi sought to reverse engineer and better understand what happens to us during flow. In his 1990 book *Flow: Psychology of the Optimal Experience*, he lays out the elements of flow, which we can read as a combination of benefits and essential ingredients.

Flow involves:

1) Complete concentration
2) Great inner clarity—knowing what needs to be done
3) Believing that the goal is attainable
4) Serenity—no worries or fear of judgment
5) Losing track of time
6) An autotelic feeling—the activity in itself must be enjoyable regardless of outcome
7) A sense of ecstasy[11]

Csikszentmihalyi's findings spawned further neurological research into what happens to our brains while we're in a state of flow. How do we enter flow? Like with meditation, can we measure its short- and long-term benefits? Most importantly, why does flow make us so happy? Is it a fleeting pleasure-like high, or a way to build true happiness worth pursuing?

What Is "Getting in the Zone"?

From a brainpower standpoint, flow sounds like someone using close to 100 percent of their brain, like Bradley Cooper's character from the movie *Limitless* (one of my favorites). There are two reasons the brain doesn't do this. The first is that using 100 percent of our brain is called having a seizure. The second is that the brain is bottlenecked by the amount of information it can process at one time, which happens to be about 110 bits of information per second. Listening to someone speak takes up 60 bits per second, which is why we can take notes during a lecture, but can't listen to two people talk at once.[12]

So on a moment-to-moment basis, what takes up most of our mental RAM? Well, the prefrontal cortex is a pretty hefty system hog. Responsible for our higher cognitive functions, the prefrontal cortex houses our social awareness, personality, sense of morality, and feelings.

Here's where flow comes in. Researchers at the American University in Beirut studied flow during exercise to find that "the extensive neural activation required to run motor patterns, assimilate sensory inputs, and coordinate autonomic regulation results in a concomitant transient decrease of neural activity in brain structures . . . that are not pertinent to performing the exercise."[13] In English, we don't use *more* of our brain during flow, we use *less*. It *shuts down* areas it doesn't need in order to channel more power to the areas in use. Any guesses which area it shuts down first?

Yup, buh-bye, prefrontal cortex. **As we engage a deeper state of flow, our self-consciousness, sense of judgment, worries, hunger, pain, even our sense of time all slip away because the brain literally stops processing them,** an effect called transient hypofrontality.

To test the power of transient hypofrontality, Australian researchers presented a tough brain teaser to forty subjects that nobody could initially solve. The researchers then artificially induced flow by suppressing the prefrontal cortex with a technique called transcranial magnetic stimulation (they shocked them with a metal donut wand). Once the subjects' minds had recovered that processing power from the prefrontal cortex, over half of them solved the brain teaser in seconds.[14]

So shutting down the prefrontal cortex is our mind's first step in engaging flow. Next, the brain releases a neural cocktail of five of the most potent chemicals it can naturally produce: serotonin, endorphins, noradrenaline, anandamide, and dopamine. The effect creates a euphoric feeling of capability, focus, confidence, creativity, and immeasurable joy. Have you ever returned from a date where you talked for hours and lost track of time? You very likely engaged flow. You *literally* created chemistry with that person. Keep their number!

These neurochemicals also dull the nervous system, reducing pain and physical sensations to further enhance focus. They super-charge the immune system as well, explaining how surfing significantly reduced the symptoms of Steven's Lyme disease.

So that's what happens to our brains on flow: we shut off parts we don't need and pour high-octane fuel on the rest. Certainly sounds like a natural feeling worth pursuing more frequently, but have scientists actually *measured* how profound the effects are?

A ten-year study conducted by McKinsey & Company found that top-ranked CEOs reported up to *five times* more productivity while in flow.[15] The Defense Advanced Research Projects Agency (DARPA) found that sniper trainees learn the intricacies of their lethal trade two to five times faster while in flow, and finally, Steven's research initiative, the Flow Genome Project, estimates that flow amplifies our sense of creativity by a factor of seven.[16]

But what if we're not looking to win a Nobel Prize, shoot through a quarter three hundred yards away, or surf into the sunset to cure a tick-borne death flu? Can we leverage flow to improve everyday life?

A Mortal's Guide to Flow

During my interviews with happy, passionate people, evidence of flow was everywhere. My buddy David, an Olympic track-and-field athlete, mentioned he often loses track of time heaving shotput after shotput. Sometimes, he even needs to set an alarm to stop himself and have dinner. Daniel, twenty-four, feels the same way on the rock wall. Soon, nothing else matters—his mind and body move as one, effortlessly calculating and gripping impossible surfaces. My cousin Claire, nineteen, often loses herself in a good book. After just a few pages, the characters spring to life in her mind, igniting her imagination as she turns page after page.

Thing is, these Millennials had *stumbled upon* flow. They recognized the feeling when I described it to them, but with the exception of the athletes and musicians, most had trouble consistently replicating it. So now that we've covered the *ingredients* of flow, what's the *recipe*?

COMET: The Flowmula

By studying the flow-rich lives of extreme athletes, Steven and his research team have extrapolated seventeen "flow triggers," detailed in his book *The Rise of Superman*. Seventeen is a lot to remember as you're trying to engage flow, so using Steven's research and my own experience, I've put together a five-point, pre-liftoff checklist for engaging flow called COMET:

1) **Challenge.** You won't engage flow playing a four-year-old in tennis or playing me in golf. Find an opponent or task that will challenge you without overwhelming you.

2) **Objective.** Is the goal to win the game? Trim the whole yard? Answer one hundred emails? Have a goal in mind as you enter flow along with a way to measure your progress, such as a percentage of completion or a score. A clear vision of progress

toward a defined goal will free the mind from higher processes such as confusion and self-doubt.

3) **Mindfulness.** Stop multitasking, put your phone away, and show respect for the present moment. Clearing out your background processes frees up your mental RAM and prepares the mind for flow.

4) **Energy.** While flow will release noradrenaline, the mind will never get there if it's fighting sleepiness. A state of wakefulness is essential; heighten your alertness with exercise, caffeine, or meditation before beginning your flow activity.

5) **Time.** Until Apple reveals the iFlow, a transcranial magnetic stimulator for numbing our prefrontal cortices, we'll have to engage flow au naturel, which takes time. With the other four ingredients present, I take around thirty minutes to engage flow while writing. Athletes and musicians I've spoken to report inducing flow in as few as ten minutes, presumably since their brain is better conditioned for it. Either way, patience and consistency is key.

Jealous of a friend's claim that she'd induced flow while *driving*, I tried applying COMET to a thirty-mile commute from my publisher's office to my house. To challenge myself, I turned off my GPS, and established the goal of getting myself home by 5:30. To stay mindful, I put my phone on airplane mode and silenced the radio. Then, with a little sip of a 5-Hour Energy, I sped down a highway entrance ramp into a churning sea of Atlanta congestion.

My first surprise was just how *quickly* I engaged flow under these conditions. With my focus narrowed by simply driving mindfully, I spotted an upcoming jam and escaped using an off ramp, navigating the twisted hills of suburban Atlanta using my internal compass. At stoplights, rather than disengage by stealing a glance at my phone, I scanned my surroundings, seeking shortcuts and landmarks. Soon I felt intensely concentrated, invigorated, and determined to best the country's ninth-worst rush hour. I was in flow.

The second surprise came after I'd arrived home at 5:24, and my sense of self-awareness returned. A mental play-by-play revealed just how much flow had changed my driving behavior. After all, I wasn't driving; *Super Chris* was, and he'd been faster, happier, kinder to other drivers, and even helped me avoid a serious accident.

Flow has helped Olympians snag gold, diplomats win negotiations, and SEALs save lives. In my life, it has helped me avoid a mindless goober in a Chevy Tahoe playing *Pokémon Go* at the wheel, and turn a rote commute into driving nirvana. So now that we've discussed the neuroscience and triggers of flow, what other flow activities should we try?

Well, flow can be achieved during just about anything that requires skill, focus, and time. To revisit some of the flow activities we've touched on, we can engage it while dancing, writing, acting, skiing, climbing, singing, boxing, painting, running, frying bacon, and almost any conceivable activity requiring focus and skill. Use COMET to experiment with some of your favorite hobbies; cut the distractions, amp the challenge, and give your mind time to enter flow.

One particular flow-inducing activity that has skyrocketed in popularity recently is coloring. In 2015 alone, sales of adult coloring books shot up from $1 million to *$12 million*. "People with a lot of anxiety respond really well to coloring books," says art therapist Nadia Jenefsky. "There are some choices involved—in terms of choosing what colors you're going to use and how you're blending your colors—but there's also a lot of structure."[17]

Coloring has flow written all over it, presenting challenging, demanding focus and skill, and providing measurable progress toward a goal. After a long day teaching kids, my friend Stephanie decompresses with a glass of red, Pandora Radio, and a fresh page in her coloring book. "I find it calming," she says, "but it still requires focus. You have to commit!" My old boss Mitch even credits coloring with reducing his blood pressure. So if you don't already have a flow activity in mind, coloring may be a great place to start.

However, unless you're Michael Phelps or Rachael Ray, swimming, cooking, and coloring aren't our jobs; they're hobbies. How about engaging flow at *work*?

Finding "the Zone" at Work

Wanda has been delivering mail to my family for nearly twenty years. While researching flow during a visit home, I heard the *clack* of closing mailboxes, so I popped outside to say hi.

"Wanda, do you like your job?"

"I better! I've been doing it for twenty years!" she chortled.

I then gave her the short version of flow and asked if she felt something like that during her route. I know my law school friends would object that I was leading the witness, but when she answered, I knew she was already a flow master.

"*Child*, I feel that every *day*. I just get into a *rhythm*!" she told me, snapping her fingers as she rocked her shoulders. "The only time I lose that good feeling is on streets with too many cars parked in my way!"

I collected similar testimony from my friend Emily in Wisconsin. She works as an assistant manager at a nice chain restaurant, sometimes up to fourteen hours per day. But she loves it. "It doesn't feel like fourteen hours. The time flies by; you feel like you're getting a lot done. Sometimes, getting out of the groove when I get home is actually kind of a letdown!"

Wanda and Emily have the advantage of being active in their jobs, without disruptions like meetings and conference calls derailing their focus. Can those of us with pseudo-sedentary office jobs leverage flow as well?

As I brought up earlier, McKinsey & Company researchers found that CEOs could achieve up to five times more productivity while in flow at work. But we don't need acre-sized offices and Ivy League business degrees to operate at their level; engaging flow at the office just requires a little strategy.

By nature, many of our jobs already provide the ingredients to COMET. We often have a goal in mind (answer one hundred emails, draft the proposal), progress is measurable, and if our jobs are a good fit, the challenges before us match our skills.

To engage flow more regularly, then, we should focus on *minimizing the impediments* to flow that typically plague an office environment. The primary culprits are (a) the urge to multitask and (b) distractions.

Tyler is a journalist for *The Atlantic* who basically lives aboard the Stress Express, constantly steamrolling toward deadlines he's unprepared for. Achieving flow has been his ace in the hole, keeping him on the payroll while his less tactful competition was swiftly weeded out. "There are times when I need to get in the zone, and I'm *almost always* able to do it."

What's his secret? Just like we created a *sleep* haven, Tyler creates a *flow* haven. "First, I gather all of the things I need to complete that specific task." That includes his laptop, notes, article clippings, and others so he won't have to interrupt flow to go find them.

Next, he makes a game plan. Since brainstorming is a higher process unfriendly to flow, Tyler ensures he enters his flow haven with the most structured plan possible. "I think about and change my mind a million times as I do the *research*, but when it's time to get it done, it's time to get in the zone."

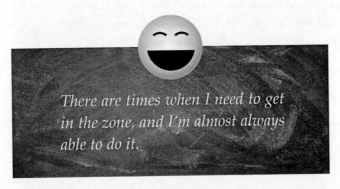

There are times when I need to get in the zone, and I'm almost always able to do it.

Lastly, he isolates himself, hiding away from officemates and putting his phone on silent. "Find a quiet, comfortable environment, and do it." Similarly, I often write with my phone on airplane mode and with noise-canceling headphones on, even if they're not playing music. Both act as neural horse-blinders, helping me maintain mindfulness and stimulating flow.

So flow is possible nearly everywhere. If we want to achieve flow more regularly, we should ask ourselves: how can we maximize COMET? Maybe our boss could give us clearer, more measurable goals so we can watch our progression. Maybe our workspace is too cluttered or noisy. Or maybe we need to ramp up the challenge!

Your Mindful Life

This week, try having a mindful meal, a mindful walk, and mindfully taking care of a few work-related to-dos. Without distractions and with respect for what you're trying to get done, things will go more quickly and pleasantly. Keep practicing, and over time, your mindful attitude will build a mindful life where you cleanly shift gears between activities and reflection, living life closer to 100 percent of your potential on a moment-to-moment basis.

Neurologically speaking, your memory, focus, and situational awareness will continue improving, and your brain will become fertile for flow, so we can become superman or superwoman more often. Through mindfulness and flow, we'll surpass our previous notions of our limits, and most importantly, our newly mindful lives will be *significantly* happier.

References:

1) "Stress in America." American Psychological Association, 2016. Accessed May 13, 2016. http://www.apa.org/news/press/releases/stress/2015/impact-of-discrimination.pdf.

2) Killingsworth, Matt. *Want to Be Happier? Stay in the Moment.* November 5, 2012. Posted September 22, 2016. https://www.ted.com/talks/matt_killingsworth_want_to_be_happier_stay_in_the_moment?language=en.

3) "Why We're Not Wired to Pay Attention to the Good Things in Life." Body & Mind. January 16, 2015. Accessed May 22, 2016. http://www.mindful.org/baby-steps-to-an-antidepressant-brain/.

4) CBS. "Eminem 60 Minutes Full Interview (2010)." *YouTube.* October 10, 2010. Posted May 22, 2016. https://www.youtube.com/watch?v=FStoecoZa88.

5) Chen, Angela. "Why Companies Are Promoting Mindfulness at the Office." *The Wall Street Journal* (wsj.com), March 16, 2015. http://blogs.wsj.com/atwork/2015/03/16/why-companies-are-promoting-mindfulness-at-the-office/.

6) Bush, Mirabai. "What's It Like to Take Google's Mindfulness Training?" *Huffington Post.* July 25, 2014. http://www.huffingtonpost.com/mirabai-bush/whats-it-like-to-take-googles-mindfulness-training_b_5617853.html.

7) *Wait Wait... Don't Tell Me!* NPR.org, April 16, 2016. Podcast.

8) Trope, Yaacov, Melissa Ferguson, and Raj Raghunathan. "Mood as a resource in processing self-relevant information." (2001).

9) Talks at Google. "Steven Kotler: 'The rise of Superman: Decoding the science of ultimate human performance.'" *YouTube*. May 5, 2014. Posted May 22, 2016. https://www.youtube.com/watch?v=y1MHyyWsMeE.

10) Csikszentmihalyi, Mihaly. *Optimal Experience: Psychological Studies of Flow in Consciousness*. Edited by Mihaly Csikszentmihalyi. Cambridge: Cambridge University Press, 1988.

11) Csikszentmihalyi, Mihaly. *Flow: The Psychology of Optimal Experience*. New York: Harper Perennial Modern Classics, 2008.

12) "Your Brain on Flow." University of Utah Health Sciences, 2012. Accessed September 27, 2016. http://healthsciences.utah.edu/innovation/state/brain-on-flow.php.

13) Dietrich, A. (2006). "Transient hypofrontality as a mechanism for the psychological effects of exercise." *Psychiatry research*, 145(1), 79–83.

14) Kotler, Steven. "Flow States and Creativity." February 25, 2014. Accessed May 27, 2016. https://www.psychologytoday.com/blog/the-playing-field/201402/flow-states-and-creativity.

15) Cranston, Susia and Scott Keller. "Increasing the 'meaning quotient' of Work." January 2013. Accessed May 22, 2016. http://www.mckinsey.com/business-functions/organization/our-insights/increasing-the-meaning-quotient-of-work.

16) Adee, Sally. "Zap Your Brain into the Zone: Fast Track to Pure Focus." February 1, 2012. Accessed May 22, 2016. https://www.newscientist.com/article/mg21328501.600-zap-your-brain-into-the-zone-fast-track-to-pure-focus?full=true.

17) Ha, Thu-Huong. "America's Obsession with Adult Coloring Is a Cry for Help." *Quartz*, April 24, 2016. http://qz.com/650378/the-sad-reason-american-adults-are-so-obsessed-with-coloring-books/.

Chapter 6 Takeaways:

- Mindfulness is the art of reengaging the present moment. It goes against our natural instinct to overthink or multitask, but pays off as we begin to fully enjoy meals, conversations, and activities.
- The brain *wants* to focus. Mindfulness improves our cognition as we process and retain more information on a moment-to-moment basis.
- To stay mindful, we should think of the present moment as a good friend and catch ourselves if we're disrespecting it by multitasking or daydreaming.
- We can initiate flow and become super-powered versions of ourselves by using COMET at work and during our favorite activities.

Up Next in Volume II of *The Millennial's Guide to Making Happiness*

Welcome to the end of Volume I! To recap what we've covered, we've broken down modern unhappiness on a macro scale, learned about the meaning of true happiness vs. pleasure, built our "happiness vehicles" through better sleep and exercise, and adopted the practices of mind and life optimization through meditation and mindfulness. Finally, we ended on a high note with flow, the most powerful mental state we can achieve. The wisdom and practices I've collected from others haven't just rescued me from the bowels of depression; they've completely reoriented my life, and I hope they serve you just as well.

On that note, remember that reading this book without taking action is like staring at a bagel when you're hungry. In order to make happiness, you must begin taking action in your own life to implement the concepts in this book. Start today. If you're not sure what action to take, refer back to the takeaways at the end of each chapter for ideas and inspiration.

Always remember, you're not alone on this happiness journey. Contact me on social media or on my website, www.chrisbutsch.com; I'd genuinely love to hear from you.

I'm thrilled to announce that *The Millennial's Guide to Making Happiness*, Volume II is already drafted, and I'm extremely excited to share it with you soon. Now that we've covered how to build happiness on your *own*, Volume II is all about optimizing your social life, honing your listening and communication skills, building your sense of compassion, becoming more altruistic, facilitating lifelong learning and passion, feeling more gratitude, understanding where money fits in, finding your dream job, and finally, finding love and the perfect life partner. You'll learn about my life-changing takeaway from a mostly silent, Illuminati-like meeting in a Memphis skyscraper, lessons learned from the worst date I've ever had, how my near-death experience in Vietnam taught me about gratitude, and how one of Atlanta's most successful wealth-management CEOs turned my idea of wealth on its head (for the better).

So while you can absolutely build a happy life with the concepts in Volume I, the rest of your life begins with your next interaction. Volume II is about mastering that interaction to maximize not only your true happiness, but the lasting happiness of those around you.

If Volume I made you laugh or helped you build happiness as I fully intended it to, I'd be so grateful if you'd now share your comments about it on social media and generally encourage others to buy a copy for themselves and for their friends and families. I'm also available for public speaking engagements, meditation training in both personal and corporate settings, and one-on-one coaching sessions or interviews via the new Carrot.FM app. For further information, and for updates regarding the upcoming releases of *ASAP Happiness: 25 Ways to Build Happiness in 5 Minutes* and *The Millennial's Guide to Making Happiness,* Volume II, please visit www.chrisbutsch.com.

I wrote this book and have dedicated my life to helping you and everyone you care about build happier lives, so I'm now humbly asking your help to spread the happiness!

Last of all, thank you so much for reading my book and joining me in the happiness revolution.

Further Research

Ten Movies about Happiness

- *Happy* (the documentary)
- *The Tiger and the Monk*
- *Amélie*
- *Hector and the Search for Happiness*
- *Secondhand Lions*
- *The Pursuit of Happyness*
- *The Peaceful Warrior*
- *Midnight in Paris*
- *Seven Years in Tibet*
- *Up in the Air*

Chris's Happiness Reading List

- *ASAP Happiness: 25 Ways to Build Happiness in 5 Minutes* by Chris Butsch
  - *The Millennial's Guide to Making Happiness* is all about building happiness over days, months, and years. But what about those little five-minute breaks throughout the day? Are there bite-sized "happiness exercises" we can do during those breaks to *build* long-term happiness? Yes! While writing this book, I've compiled twenty-five of them, with anecdotal and scientific support, in a quick, fun-to-read eBook, coming soon to Amazon and iBooks. For

updates, please subscribe to my blog at www.chrisbutsch.com.

- *Flow* by Mihaly Csikszentmihalyi
  - My favorite positive-psychology book. Like a modern philosopher, Csikszentmihalyi (cheek-sent-me-high) accurately predicted much of what the scientists in this book would later confirm using fMRI scans. Plus, his book has a chapter called Cheating Chaos. Enough said.
- *How to Win Friends and Influence People* by Dale Carnegie
  - I bought this book for my stepbrother and told him I wouldn't drop him off at college until he read it. It's that critical for being an effective interpersonal communicator, which in turn is essential for happy living.
- *Never Eat Alone* by Keith M. Ferrazzi
  - A book about why you should master the art of networking, and how. It helped me build and maintain a wide network of friends and connections, many of whom made this book possible.
- *10% Happier* by Dan Harris
  - *Nightline* anchorman Dan Harris recounts how his equivalent to the Rock Star Lifestyle led him to have an on-air panic attack, and how his skeptical journey through religious practices led him to become one of meditation's greatest advocates. This book is the cure for meditation skepticism.
- *Happiness* by Thich Nhat Hanh
  - *Happiness* is like a field manual for Buddhist mindfulness practices. If you're interested in visiting a monastery or learning more about the daily lives of Buddhist monks, it's a quick, essential read.

- *Play* by Stuart Brown
  - All about the neuroscience and importance of fun. It's an easy, quick read; blitz through it in a couple of sittings and reconnect with your inner child.
- *Mindfulness as Medicine* by Sister Dang Nghiem
  - Written by "Sister D" of Magnolia Grove Monastery, *Mindfulness as Medicine* recounts her incredible, heart-wrenching, pre-monastic life from the Tet Offensive in Vietnam to her penniless migration, her career as a doctor, and a sorrowful love story inspiring her to join the monkhood. Her story stands testament to the power of a mindful life.
- *Search Inside Yourself* by Chade-Meng Tan
  - Google's self-help bible. Penned by their former "Jolly Good Fellow," *Search Inside Yourself* is a goofy, fun guide to mindful living peppered with silly illustrations and good advice.
- *Choose the Life You Want* by Tal Ben-Shahar
  - A highly addictive collection of 101 bite-sized happiness tips. Perfect for stockings and coffee tables.
- *Emotional Intelligence 2.0* by Travis Bradberry
  - Shortly into this book you'll take a Myers-Briggs-like test online that scores four aspects of your emotional intelligence: self-awareness, self-management, social awareness, and relationship management. The rest of the book consists of ways to improve all four. I fell a bit short in social awareness, so the book helped me become more mindful of others' emotions.

Acknowledgments

Without the following friends, family, colleagues, and friendly sages, this book wouldn't have been possible. Thank you all so, so much!

- Jan Schroder
- Tom Butsch
- Jorge and Catherine Butsch Villareal
- Vicky, Ryan, and Samantha Boyce
- Chris and Thomas Schroder
- Hill Schroder
- Bob Richey
- Chris, Claire, and Kate Richey
- David Butsch, Henry Butsch, and Laura Butsch
- The monks of Magnolia Grove Monastery, especially Sister D and Brother Harmony
- Mark Kagika, Julian White, Roman Uzhachenko
- Matt Thomas, Leigh Ann McKinley, Joseph Hodges, and Rosalee Lewis
- James Lee Henley, Shawn Ellis, Will Nichols, Thomas Idzik, Gavin Grishom, and Matt Huhman
- Karsten Aichholz
- Ryan Buck, Dave Buck, and Stephanie Anna
- Steven Sanders and Lyndsey Loveberry
- John Whittemore and the members of Vicious Writers Circle Atlanta
- Everyone at Buckhead Toastmasters, especially Kat Minnifield
- My China crew, especially Jennifer Taylor, Siobhan Clare Keane, Jennifer Taylor, Matthew Dolan, Pat Neary, Holly

Braithwaite, and Tar Dai for contributing to this book and its sequel
- My Vietnam crew, especially Michele Castillo and Dang Nguyen
- Erin Tyler, my brilliant cover designer
- Sherri Nadeau
- Edy Kauan
- Spencer Vereen
- Celia Quillian
- Henry Faber
- Maria Valdes
- Charlie Hoehn
- Palmer Greene and Robbie Ottley
- Elena Villa
- Cameron Stewart and James Marshall
- Rob Bednarski and Sebastian Norrdahl
- Ryan Stutler and Joe Barbato
- Andrew Kenner and Kayla Griffin
- Melissa Allen Heath
- The crew at Atmasphere Buckhead, especially Pavel and Howie
- Andrew Holzhauer
- Kian Jelly

I'd also like to thank those who were especially generous to my Kickstarter campaign, and helped make this book possible:

- Betty Ann and Larry Abblitt
- Ted and Graciela Ansusinha
- Jordan Baltes
- Libby Barnard
- Judy and Roberts Bass
- Robert Bednarski
- Claudia Beltran
- Beth and Alison Beskin

- Vicky, Ryan, and Samantha Boyce
- Susan Boyd
- Charlie and Mary Katherine Brake
- Jill Brennan
- Lisa and William Bridges
- Veronica Brown
- Meg Buker
- Chris Burnett
- Rick Butsch
- David and Laura Butsch
- "Big" Rick Butsch
- Steve and Margo Butsch
- Candis Carpenter
- Evan Carter
- Michele Castillo and Sean Perez
- Victor Clarke
- The Cronk Family
- Sissy and Brian Dabid
- Margaret and Dallas Denny
- Gerrome Diadula
- Matthew Dolan
- The Egan Family
- Elizabeth Elliott
- Shawn Ellis
- Louise Faurot
- Sally Finch
- Beth Finnerty and David Martin
- Avery Fisher
- David Geller
- Natalie Gow
- Chris and Silvana Grigaluans
- Joy Hannemann
- Haley Helveston
- Joseph Hodges
- Caroline Howell

- Donna Hunter
- Greg and Anne Kala
- Edy Kauan
- Beth and Bruce Kempe
- Andrew Kenner
- Richard and Sandy Kessler
- Marika King
- The Klugman Family
- Johnny Lai
- Deborah Lanham
- Shana Lombardi
- Michelle Lynn
- Laura Mangham
- Leigh Ann McKinley
- Elizabeth Morgan
- Susan and Tom Murphy
- Matthew Nickerson
- Krassimir Nikov
- David and Laura Nix
- Sebastian Norrdahl
- Jack O'Leary
- Stephen Opler
- Marco "Juicy J" Patrie
- Ollie Patterson
- Graham Perry
- Quan Trong Pham
- Robert Pue
- Anastasiia Pylypiuk
- Matthew Quadrini
- Silviu Raducu
- Chris, Claire, and Kate Richey
- Greg and Connor Richey
- Bill and Alyssa Roberts
- Jenny Rocks
- Michael and Martiele Schroder

- Caryl and Ken Smith
- Tiwa Soyebo
- Don Stormo
- Claire and Dustin Stovall
- Matthew John Thomas
- Tonya and Chuck Veal
- Cristina Villarreal
- Rogelio and Irma Villarreal
- Jorge and Catherine Butsch Villarreal
- John and Jennifer Waddy
- Chadwick Wade
- Robroy Wiley
- Brandon Williams
- Robert Wilson
- Adam Wilson
- Patti and Nick Wolfcale
- Dennis and Martie Zakas

My Happiness Heroes

- The Broyles Family
- Christina Chaplin
- Thomas Idzik
- Christopher Oppermann
- Steve and Lyndsey Sanders

My Happiness Champions

- Tom and Vicky Butsch
- Jan and Chris Schroder
- Jorge and Catherine Butsch Villarreal

Index

About the Author

Chris Butsch is an author, speaker, meditation instructor, and Millennial Happiness Expert. At age twenty-five, he left a stable career in IT project management to study happiness with the ultimate goal of reversing America's slipping happiness levels, starting with his own generation. Chris has written three books on happiness and regularly trains others how to meditate in his hometown of Atlanta, Georgia. He has been called "The Malcolm Gladwell of Happiness" and "sexy Mark Zuckerberg."